PASTORAL PRAYERS
for the
CHURCH YEAR

PASTORAL PRAYERS
for the
CHURCH YEAR

by

SAMUEL JOHN SCHMIECHEN

ABINGDON PRESS
NEW YORK • NASHVILLE

TO
Marie

PREFACE

The importance of the pastoral prayer in Protestant worship cannot be overemphasized. It may be the high moment of worship. Certainly through it windows of the soul are often opened by which other portions of the service are viewed with fresh and new meaning. By following the Church Year the great truths of the Christian faith may be related vividly, regularly, and naturally to the experience of the people who are constantly exposed to the distracting rounds of the secular. Why should not the best and the most intimate of the past and of the present be used to express the language, rhythm, and music which belong to the heart communing with the Eternal?

Prayers gain vibrancy and effectiveness as they voice specific moods, concerns, and aspirations in the language of today. The pastor who is acquainted with his flock will know how to speak as a shepherd in its behalf. On the other hand, the immeasurable wealth of insight, inspiration, beauty, and experience contained within the holy conversation of Christians with their God, preserved through the centuries, would be denied to worshipers if the pastor's own prayers were used exclusively. Even at best, the inevitable monotony and limitations of a single source of prayers would be deadening to the congregation which has a right to feel the winds of the living Spirit which have blown across the faces of many generations that lifted up their hearts to God. It is impossible to acknowledge my indebtedness for phrases from poetry, Scripture, and classic prayers of the past or present, which memory and experience have joined into enriching overtones.

These prayers were written with the worship and life of a congregation in mind. They are being submitted to the public with the hope that they may become contemporary testimony that God touches with the breath of his Spirit the spiritual tendrils of an ordinary minister and his people. These prayers were alternately used with the treasury of prayers which the Christian Church has gleaned through the centuries. Lay leaders may find portions of the pastoral prayers and the special prayers helpful in guiding groups in worship.

A word of highest appreciation must be expressed to the members of St. Paul's Evangelical and Reformed Church, St. Paul, Minnesota, in whose Christian fellowship these prayers were conceived and spoken. This little collection of prayers came into being largely through the encouragement of my colleague, Dr. Erwin R. Koch, with whom I have been privileged to serve as co-pastor during five happy years. The gladsome spirit and strong faith which Dr. Koch and his wife, Rita, have shared in bright and dark hours is an inspiration to all of us who know them. Further encouragement also came from my brothers, the Rev. Siegfried Schmiechen and the Rev. Kurt Schmiechen, who frequently spurred me into action. I am especially indebted to my brother Kurt for carefully reading and correcting the manuscript.

All three of us brothers often speak with affection and gratitude for our parents, Elizabeth Schmiechen and the late Rev. Reinhold Schmiechen, who inspired the fervency and beauty of our first prayers. My wife, Marie, has shared more than I can tell here of precious things which have inclined me to pray and cause me to give thanks to God. She is a devoted mother to our three children—Daniel, Peter, and Abigail. In addition to being a gifted helpmate, she has carefully typed the entire manuscript.

If these prayers encourage someone to pray or to write his own prayers and point to the Father of our Lord Jesus Christ, whose Spirit moves among us today as surely as in the days of old, I shall be profoundly thankful.

SAMUEL JOHN SCHMIECHEN

CONTENTS

VI. Special Prayers

I

Invocations ~~10/13/57~~

1

O God everlasting, whose beauty dawns in the morning, whose glory shines at noonday, and whose loveliness appears at eventide; we hunger and thirst after thy goodness. No beauty satisfies until we know thy holiness; no life gains fullest joy until blessed by the fairest love of our Saviour; no glory abides until we know life eternal. In our adoration help us to see what we have overlooked or lost. In our hearing of the Word, give us open minds and obedient wills. As we seek thy face, grant us power to become known as thine, to whom alone belongeth honor and praise; through Jesus Christ our Lord. AMEN.

2   ~~3/2/58~~

O God, whom we know as our Father through our Lord Jesus Christ; with thee is the fountain of life, and in thy light shall we see light. Let thy Spirit, dwelling richly in Christ, draw us to his life and truth. Stir our hearts with awe and faith, that in receiving and giving we may increase in love and courage. May our common needs which bring us to this hour cause us to pray one for another and to witness more devotedly in the fellowship of thy Church universal; through Jesus Christ our Lord. AMEN.

3

God our Father, whose mercy is filled with strength and joy; let not our weakness or sadness of spirit keep thee from blessing us in this worship. Arouse us from self-pity and despair to the consciousness that our lives are thine. Thy face is over us; thou art able to inspire hearts; thou speakest an eternal word. May thy presence be so real that through this service we may go in thy ways with confidence and gladness; through Jesus Christ our Lord. AMEN.

4

10/25/59

O God, whose Spirit searches our hearts and reveals the life of thy kingdom; take from us all dullness of conscience, all lukewarmness of heart, and all callousness of spirit. Fill us with a yearning for thy forgiveness and with a holy desire to know thee as thou truly art. We would place all stubbornness and pride of spirit at the foot of thine altar. Help us to look up to thy cross, that we may behold the wisdom and love that saves; through Jesus Christ our Lord. AMEN.

5

O God of heaven and earth, who comest to every lowly soul; thy Spirit alone makes our worship a blessing. Let those of us who come to thee with wounded hearts find healing; may those who are possessed of joy give unto thee the glory. To those who are rebellious in spirit, reveal the crucified Christ. Unto those who seek wisdom, disclose thy truth. To all of us grant thy mercies in our need to be forgiven. Let this holy hour link our striving with thy will, our weakness with thy strength, and our souls with the beauty of thy peace; through Jesus Christ our Lord. AMEN.

6

Almighty God our Father, thou hast created the first day of our world and every gift-laden hour of our lives. We praise

14

thee for this day in which things eternal promise to dawn upon us. We would adore thee in joyous worship as thy Spirit refreshes us. Let this holy day recall that thou livest and reignest over life and death. We long with all believers for thy Word that can create order, beauty, and strength of soul. Through its power we would live in hope among the fleeting days of this earth and prepare for that glorious day when all things shall be new; through Jesus Christ our Lord. AMEN.

7

Eternal God, by whose wisdom the worlds were fashioned, through whose life we were created, and in whose love is our salvation; we praise thee for this day of thanksgiving and dedication. As thou hast given light and knowledge in the past, so lead us by thy grace into paths of promise and fulfillment. Make us heirs of the devotion of the faithful and redeemed. Glorious are thy ways, O Lord, in the midst of our weakness and strength, our failures and accomplishments. We rejoice in all thy mercies. Help us to lay hold of the truth of the gospel, inviting us to life in thy name; through Jesus Christ our Lord. AMEN.

II

A Confession of Sins

8

O God, who in loving righteousness comest near to us in our sinful thoughts and ways, whose holiness searches the heart and whose goodness confronts our unworthiness; we confess before thee our transgressions: we have lived as if life were our own; we have used thy blessings without discerning their purpose; our ungratefulness has often emptied life of its joys; by our indifference thy work has waited; because we have not loved thee with our whole heart, other hearts have not been drawn to thee; we have harbored low desires which kept us from seeing lives as thou dost see them; we have spoken hasty and cruel words when the law of kindness should have ruled our lips; we have been angry with a brother and asked for patience for ourselves; we have judged the weakness of others when we were in the same condemnation; evil imagination has darkened our spirits. Thou knowest, O Lord, our littleness of faith and our lack of love. Father, we are deeply sorry for our debts of the soul and implore thee by the mercy and the power that was in Christ to forgive us our sins and to cleanse us from all evil. Keep us close to thee in faith, love, and desire that by thy grace we may rise worthily as sons and daughters of thine, brothers and sisters one of another; through Jesus Christ our Lord. AMEN.

III

Prayers of Intercession

7/20/58

9

O God, who in Christ didst teach us to pray one for another; we do not always know how to pray for those whom we love. Bestow upon them blessings which we cannot give because of our weakness and partial judgment. May they enjoy what is truly good for them. Let our own mistakes and shortcomings be understood by them in the light of the best gifts we covet earnestly for them. In time of danger give them courage and protection. When tempted let faith's sight help them to look beyond the hollow allurement of evil. Let them see the invitations to the things that are pure, lovely, and of good report. Confirm them in every holy desire and noble purpose. When they are far from us, keep them close to thy heart; through Christ our Lord. AMEN.

10

Our Father, who thinkest of all and rememberest their need; we would also pray for those whom we have in mind. Keep strong all who watch over the sick—doctors, nurses, counselors, and technicians. Guard all who protect us from enemies and corruption, from fire and pestilence. Lift the spirit of discouragement from those who labor at monotonous tasks. Give to all leaders knowledge of the common welfare. Let brightness of hope beam upon all who are enshrouded in sorrow. Send vision to all teachers and students. Alert those who are working in dangerous places. Let the enjoyment of thy nearness be the reward of those who do good in secret. May those who suffer for their sins come to repentance and find the offers of restoring grace. Give to all who write and speak, wisdom and judgment to prove all things and to hold fast to that which is good. Aid those who champion truth among the ways of the people. To all who would inspire, grant a full portion of thy Spirit; in the name of him who lifts up every heart, even Jesus Christ. AMEN.

11 4/27/58

O Christ, who hast taught us to pray for our enemies; take away any spirit of vengeance so that we may ask for them the good things we desire for ourselves. Make us like-minded to do justly, love mercy, and walk humbly before thee. Give us the grace to see one another no longer separately but as bound together with thee in Christ. Let our love be so genuine that through the spirit that was in Christ we may overcome evil with good; in his name. AMEN.

IV

Offertory Prayers

12

God our Father, who in wise providence hast bountifully prepared gifts for every portion of our life; we thank thee that with each blessing thou dost grant us the power to love and to share. May our offering be a sign of grateful lives, bound together in faith and service; through Jesus Christ our Lord. AMEN.

13

Gracious God, who in Christ hast revealed the meaning of our lives and who through thy Holy Spirit dost share those influences of faith which make us thine; grant now the greatest of all gifts, the gift of love to accompany these offerings, transforming them into a power for good in thy kingdom; through Jesus Christ our Lord. AMEN.

14

O God, who alone canst bless us; grant that with the deeds of our hands the blessings of the Spirit may follow, with the words of our mouths the understanding of the heart may abide, with the inspiration of this hour true service may go forth, and in our dedication before thine altar we may follow thee in daily discipleship; through Jesus Christ our Lord. AMEN.

15

O God, who in Christ art Lord of our life and who through him hast freely given us all things; we give gladly this offering, for thou art our joy; we see our lives as thine and are thankful; we hear thee calling us to be laborers in the harvest of thy kingdom and praise thee that we may find life by losing it for thy sake; through the same Jesus Christ our Lord. Amen.

16

Our Father, who in Christ hast taken us into partnership with thyself in the work of thy kingdom; help us to see that every material gift was bestowed to bless some life; each trust placed in our keeping must be accounted for in the light of love for our fellow man. Inspire us to be good stewards that our faithfulness in this life may become our joy and reward in the life to come; to the honor of thy holy name. Amen.

17

Praise be unto thee, O God, for good things given to us without our working for them, for mercies offered to us without our deserving them, and for the love of Christ for us even when we loved not in return. Through these offerings we acknowledge that we are debtors to thee and to our fellow man. Grant us now the joy of giving with thankful hearts and for thy sake; through Jesus Christ our Lord. Amen.

18

O God everlasting, whose kingdom has come to this world in Christ; we thank thee that in the midst of possessions which moth and rust corrupt, we may lay up treasures that abide. Through faith and love transform our gifts and our talents into possessions of the Spirit. So may they enrich life in the kingdom and glorify thee, our Father in heaven; through Jesus Christ our Lord. AMEN.

19

O Christ, who hast called us into the service of thy church; open our eyes to the needs which thou beholdest in the world. Then grant us compassionate hearts and willing hands, that what thou commandest will become our joy and what we accomplish will be to thy honor and glory to the ends of thy kingdom. In thy name we ask it. AMEN.

20

Lord of all mercy, who freely givest us all things in Jesus Christ; help us to remember that to whom much is given, of him much will be required. Let our membership in thy church and our giving to thy work be honest and faithful to the measure in which thou dost prosper, that the gospel may abound unto many waiting hearts; through Jesus Christ our Lord. AMEN.

V

For the Church Year and Special Days

21

ADVENT PREPARATION

O God, who reignest in a kingdom that is and is to come, and who hast placed a desire in our hearts that leaves us seekers until we find thee; let this Advent become a season of glad awaiting of thee in our worship and life together. We long for thee even when we know it not. We praise thee, God of our fathers, that as thou hast revealed thyself through the ages, so thy Spirit invades our day and opens new ways for thy coming to our souls. Dwell among our hurried and dissatisfied lives until we recognize thee as the fulfillment of our spirits' groping and longing.

Impart to us a clear vision of faith like that of the patriarchs by which paths toward thy kingdom are blazed. Lead us to discover the law which thou didst write upon the heart. Attune our spirits that we may hear the voice of the Redeemer of whom the prophets spoke. Awaken us to a high expectancy, because thy promises to us are as abundant and gracious as in the days of old.

O Saviour-Messiah, who makest preparation for every new coming of thine into the events of the world; let our preparation to welcome thee be sincere and complete. Make us quick to surrender and cast out what thou wilt not bless.

When thou comest in judgment of our sins, give us contrite hearts. When thou wilt not sanction our attitudes, give us courage to come to the place where thou standest. As thou enterest our homes, unite our families in the peace and understanding of love. Make thou this sanctuary a holy place and take away our uncertainty and weariness. We would behold thee all lovely, like the dawning splendor of the morning after the darkness of night.

Lord, who comest to comfort thy people; be thou the consolation of the aged. Come as a guiding vision to those who stand in the struggles of the day. Direct the searching eyes of youth until they find and follow thee. May those in our land or in distant countries who are waiting for the hour of redemption receive sufficient assurance through outward signs and inward miracles that none wait and pray in vain.

Now let us go forth as thy servants who are unafraid of the world because thou art in the midst of it, and rejoice in the good tidings of an eternal kingdom; through Jesus Christ our Lord. AMEN.

22

ADVENT LIGHT

O God our Father, whom no eye of man hath seen and who dwellest in the light of eternal glory; we praise thee for the light of the knowledge of thy glory in the face of Jesus Christ. Thine is the power we need. Thine are the gifts by which we are saved. Thou art the Morning Star, standing in the midst of nights of waiting and sighing of the spirits of men. We thank thee for all who trusted thy leading in the storms of history, for all who bravely proclaimed the gospel of the kingdom, and for all who have endured persecution and disfavor for thy sake.

Merciful God, remember not our having loved darkness

better than the lamp of an everlasting Word. We confess that our eyes have been turned by the gleam of worldly possessions, by flashing lust, by fleeting pleasures, and by foolish pretensions. We have watched the flickering lights of human wisdom and turned away from the Sun of Righteousness. In our hasty selfish steps we have neglected the health of our souls. In our self-pity we have lost our sympathy for others. Holy Light of our lives, burn out the dross of our sin and forgive us.

O Spirit of God, make the flame of our conscience shine steadily against evil winds, lest it falter and go out. Illumine the places where thou desirest us to serve. We would join hands in thy world-wide Church that all men may come to the knowledge of the truth. Light thou the candle of our spirit that it may burn with the calmness of faith, with the fragrance of love, and in purity of heart.

O thou Giver of life, who hearest the low cry of humanity; we remember thee in Christ as bowing over those bent in grief and shame. Reveal thy salvation to all races, tongues, and nations. Bless with mercy all who are bereft of the light of reason. Let the aged and helpless feel thy tender care. Bring the consolation of thy kingdom to all who sit in the darkness of sorrow, in prison, or in the shadow of death. Come, O God, to thy church and to all thy children, in old and new ways, until we behold thy glory in never-fading light; through Jesus Christ our Lord. Amen.

23

ADVENT HOPE

Everlasting God, who in Jesus Christ givest assurance to every heart that hopes in thee; grant us such certainty of mind and spirit that we may worship, labor, and pray as those who love thy appearing. Thou art a strong Deliverer;

therefore we, like the psalmist, would sing songs of praise though gloom surround us. They who have trusted in thee have never been put to shame; therefore we have confidence for our day. Permit us to see the evidences of thy healing and redeeming power that we may lift up our hearts. In our highest moments of insight we see thee in a land that is afar off where peace and righteousness dwell and for which the ages have waited. As we search the Scriptures, we find thee near in him of whom the prophets spoke. Our hearts exult with an old and ever-new joy in thy Son, who comes to our humanity to befriend us with divine mercy. Blessed art thou, O Christ.

O King of life, free us from the slavery of sins which have a grip upon our wills. Make us bold in the certainty of the good and true which is to prevail. May thy advent in the events of our time drive away our anxiety, our false hopes, and our selfish ambition. Take from us all hate, uncharitableness, and bitterness. Melt the hardness of our hearts and brighten our vision until we know thee as the eternal Hope that is among us. We wait patiently for thee, our Father; renew our strength to walk as thy children.

O brightest Promise from God, awaken a new surge of trust-filled devotion in thy church. Aid us to find and express the spirit of love and of generosity in our Christmas preparations. Give to our disconsolate world the peace that is built upon righteous good will and brotherly sympathy. Bless all who are stricken by grief with the hope of eternal life. Permit all who bear sickness to feel the restoring power of thy hand.

O Lord, Hope of the world; give us an upward look that sweeps beyond the drudgery and hardship of the day. Keep us faithful in our appointed tasks until thou comest to vanquish the reign of evil and to establish thy kingdom in power and glory; through Jesus Christ our Lord. AMEN.

24

THE COMING OF GOD
(*Advent*)

Almighty God our Father, who art our Maker and our Friend, our Judge and our Saviour; thy presence moves through all creation and pauses before each waiting heart. Before we were a life or needed anything, thou didst prepare in love for each of us. Give us the grace to behold how thou art reigning anew in our age and hast control of the days before us. Thou art always ready to listen to each contrite and humble spirit. Thou standest against the footsteps of evil like a high wall of righteousness. Our perplexing troubles cannot elude thy divine wisdom and compassion. Let not familiarity with holy things, seen and unseen, close our will and understanding to the wonder of thy love in Jesus Christ. We adore and praise thee for visiting each of us, O divine Guest.

We thank thee that thou comest to meet us as we are. Come then to our sinning and stumbling lives, our Father. Free us from the slavery of impure desires and evil deeds. Thou art standing among us with strength to redeem. Thou canst make all things new. Show us what lies beyond our regrets, our sorrows, and our scars. We would go with thee, O Friend of sinners, to meet the true Source of our humanity in the Christ Child. Through a miracle of faith and love claim us. Then will we awaken from sin, ready to offer ourselves to thy high calling, O God.

Unite thy church in the unity that is in Christ, in which manifold gifts enrich fellowship and strengthen faith. Confront us as members of the many races of mankind, our Father, and inspire us to serve thee as one family. Move the assembly of nations to heed thy laws and judgments so that none may honor their own nation more than the welfare

26

of all people. Give us courage to commend the peace of the gospel of Christ.

O God, who outrunnest us and pursuest us with the Spirit of the kingdom of love and righteousness; break down our crooked reasoning and all foolish trusting in the ways and institutions of men. Come, O refreshing Spirit, which was and is in Christ, and raise us to a season of holy receiving and giving; through Jesus Christ our Lord. AMEN.

25

CHRISTMAS EVE

Everlasting Father, whose glorious love and holy righteousness appeared in Jesus Christ; we adore thee for this night of fulfillment and rejoicing. As we behold the wonder of thy goodness, we bow in humility and repentance. The innocence of the Babe rebukes our selfishness, hardness, and unbrotherliness. Forgive us our sins. We would make room in our hearts for thy presence by letting evil be driven out and thy Spirit be born anew. Then shall we know the gifts of thy peace and good will.

O God, who by thy incarnation art always ready to let miracles of grace invade our dull lives; we praise thee for the songs of Christmas and their melodies of faith, for our homes and the spirit of trust and affection, for friends and their kindness, for every generous impulse through which the needy are given gladness, and for the hopes wherein heaven's truths draw near to comfort and bless.

Gentle Son of God, who didst come to us as a Saviour; quicken our faith in thy redeeming power that still walks unseen the dusty roadways of the world. Help us to live and work by the memory of thy tenderness and might, which we behold in Bethlehem and on the cross. In this thy light of love may we not only give of our substance but commit ourselves wholly to thee.

As we kneel in awe before the manger, we would name all dear ones, that thou mayest grant unto each thine unspeakable gift in Christ. May those who have not yet seen the Christmas star follow thy Spirit's leading until they find the wonder of thy love.

O thou who art the King of love and life, be thou our Lord and Guide while we follow in faith, until all men learn to serve together as brothers and as sons of one Father in heaven. Thine shall be the glory; through Jesus Christ our Lord. AMEN.

26

THE OLD YEAR

O God, who art from age to age the same and whose presence is ever new among the passing years; we lift up grateful hearts for thy manifold blessings during this year now drawing to a close. Thou hast never forgotten us. With patience didst thou await our return when we wandered from thee. Thou hast opened thy hands in mercy, and we have received boundless compassion, pardon, and joy. The passing hours are even as the generations of men that come and go. Yet each moment numbers the procession of good things which have enlarged and enriched our lives.

We thank thee for our church and her leaders, and for the countless believers who have upheld Christian hands at work with gifts and prayer. Thou hast inspired minds to reflect thy thoughts and to draw us from evil toward good. Thy Word has not returned unto us void, and within its pages we have discerned the story of salvation. Dear ones have trusted us when we did not trust ourselves. They have wooed us with love until we found thee in their hearts. In hard tasks we found the strength of the Spirit; our short-sighted requests received gifts far better than our prayers. For all these signs of the working of Christ's Spirit, we raise our song in triumph and praise.

O Christ, we confess our needless ignorance and slowness to learn, our waste of time and talents, our reluctant witness for the gospel, and our hasty condemnation of others. We would not go hence, O Lord, until thou dost bless us with forgiveness. Open the windows of our imagination to holy insights. Fill our hearts with faith and our hands with worthy work until our life becomes a sacrament in thy sight. Thou who knowest all things, accompany us upon unknown ways lest we falter. Give us grace to sit in sympathy with the homeless, oppressed, and sick of the world. As another year returns to thy eternity, let thine everlasting arms uphold us as we welcome the new year into our vows and labors. Now bless our going out and our coming in; through Jesus Christ who is the same yesterday, today, and forevermore. AMEN.

27

THE NEW YEAR

Lord, who hast been our dwelling place in every generation, before whom all lives are judged in righteousness and everlasting mercy; be thou our Guide and Desire of life in the days before us. Thy breath of life sustains us. Bless unto us each joy and sorrow, and all light and darkness with thy gracious providence.

We tremble in the midst of our hurrying days; grant us an awareness that each life is long enough to love and be loved, that every face was meant to be turned unto thee, and that every heart was formed to beat with brotherly concern. Eternal God, in this New Year let our frail lives give evidence of the power of thy love and the strength of thy

Spirit. May our brief hours and days be markers of joy, of kindness, and of a deathless faith.

O God our Father, who watchest over all thy children; release us from fruitless anxieties born out of our uncertainties. Our days pass away as the grass of the field. Help us to face life with thee, O Christ. Then we shall be free from self-pity and fear, and confident that abiding strength shall be sufficient for us.

In this New Year make us even as thy candle, O Lord. Replenish us with courage to illumine the things which belong to thy kingdom. Give us patience to wait until thou art ready to bless. In all the events and experiences before us, direct our eyes to look not to man but to thee.

Bless each of us now as we lay down the stained pages of our lives and by thy grace ask for the clean whiteness of thy forgiveness.

O thou who rulest over governments, peoples, and nations; crown us with thy lovingkindness in this New Year and lead us into thine everlasting kingdom; through Jesus Christ our Lord. Amen.

28

EPIPHANY

Everlasting God our Father, who art the Inspirer of the song of youth, the Giver of hope to the mature, and the Answer to the yearnings of the aged; in thee do we find fulfillment in our journey of faith. Each generation is blessed as it adventures in doing thy will. As we test the old and the new, we rejoice that Christ's words still echo thy eternal truth. We would carry with us the joyous tidings that Christ was born the Saviour of the world.

Match our souls to the times wherein we live. We hear the heroes of the kingdom calling us to perfect that which they began and for which they endured. When evil men seek to dethrone the truth, make us to be brave defenders of justice and love. Keep us patient in trial, generous among the needy, courageous in defeat, and humble in our privileges. Make us to be messengers of hope to thy children of this torn earth.

Raise up men and women who in the spirit of Christ will bring the fullness and power of the gospel to the north and south, the east and west. Save the young people of all lands from blind guides and reveal thyself to them as the Light of life. Fill them with such love for thee that they may accept Christ's invitation to enter the kingdom. Empower the peoples of all nations to put down the legions of darkness and strife. Stir up every gift among them for common deliberation and effort until righteousness and peace follow their ways.

Our Father, who dost open for us new and different ways, and dost accompany us to bestow heaven-laden gifts; grant us vision and steadfastness to walk as thy loving children. So may the things we hoped and worked for by thy grace be remembered and completed by those who follow us when our earthly way ends at the open door of the eternal kingdom; through Jesus Christ our Lord. AMEN.

29

WINTER PRAISE

Almighty and merciful God, whose splendor shines in each ray of light and who through the love of thy dear Son Jesus Christ countest every tear; we adore thee for the beauty and compassion of thy Spirit among us. As white snowflakes cover the earth with soft loveliness from the heavens, so thy innumerable providences bless our souls. As winter artistry covers familiar scenes with beauty, so thou canst adorn us with the comeliness that is of our Saviour. Behold the barrenness of our lives! Permit the light of comfort to shine upon sorrow born of death, and make the light of hope to shine upon sorrow born of sin. Cover our stained spirits with a new cleanness and goodness.

Thou art our shelter when cold winds of unbelief and bitterness blow. Thou art like the everlasting hills towering above the storms. Thy Spirit speaks to us like the stillness of a clear night. Our voices would join in a song of praise for thy winter beauty and for thy splendor of goodness that is in Christ.

We thank thee also, our Father, for these days in which we are bound together intimately in the warmth of home and church, with kindred and friends. We are grateful for all who minister to our comfort, safety, and health. Evoke in us daily appreciation for the tender care of human love. We thank thee for unselfish parents, for the love that binds husband and wife, for the trust of little children, and for friends who enrich us with counsel and companionship. Teach us to enlarge the joys of imagination and memory. Help us to find the treasures that await us in literature, in music, and in art. Awaken us for growth in grace through work and play. Bless us in our conversation and prayer by the hearthside.

Great God, in this holy hour remember in lovingkindness all for whom we pray: those who are bringing the ministry of healing to sick bodies and minds, all who labor faithfully at appointed tasks at lonely posts or among moving multitudes. Make thy church a friendly shelter for the spiritually hungry and homeless. For those to whom death brings terrifying thoughts, let the seeds of immortal hope in Christ become buds of faith that shall blossom forth unto an eternal springtime.

Now may thy loving Spirit, which dwelt so richly in him who is our Lord, subdue our selfishness and set us free to serve thee in season and out of season; to whom alone belongeth honor and glory forevermore. AMEN.

30

INTERNATIONAL MISSIONS

God our Father, who in Christ art the Saviour of the world; arouse thou faith in our hearts as we look upon the troubled peoples of every nation. Thy sovereign might prevails in the midst of the powers and forces of our day. Still thou art bringing the order of truth and life to thy world. Thou art our Father, and all of us are thy children, created in thine image. What we have forgotten, thou rememberest forever; where we have hated, thou wouldst love; where we have destroyed, thou wouldst redeem; where souls are lost, thou art seeking until they return; where ignorance and superstition darken the mind, thou art ready to bring the light of life; where sickness lays low the bodies and minds of men, thou wouldst bring healing in thy wings. O Redeemer of the race of men, by thy mercy save us from our sins and make us whole again as thy family on earth and in heaven.

We remember with gratitude all messengers of thy Word who through stormy seas and perilous paths brought the gospel to our fathers. Without this precious heritage we could not this hour rejoice in the gift of thy life and love. Bestow upon us strength and courage that our faith and deeds may become a consistent witness unto all who watch our ways. May those who love thee not be persuaded by thy truth and those who know thee not find in Christ life's deepest thirst satisfied. Impart to us the world-wide vision of the Spirit which belongs to thy disciples.

O God, whose Spirit calls us to serve in thy kingdom; we utter our praise for the work of our missionaries in many lands. We are grateful that through them our devotion to thee may bear fruit. Be especially near to those who because of persecution are suffering imprisonment or hardship. By thy grace let the upheavals and confusions of the peoples in our time become a means unto the furtherance of the gospel of him who loved us and gave himself for us.

Aid those beginning their labors to enter with confidence and joy the fields where others have planted and watered. Awaken many hearts by the preaching and teaching in the name of a living Lord. Inspire doctors and nurses in the midst of exhausting demands and physical dangers. May the sick and wounded find the cure of souls as they receive healing for their bodies. Direct those who teach the stewardship of soil and the mastery of science so that all may earn daily bread and walk with the dignity of sons and daughters of God.

Bless thou the growth of native churches and enlarge the wisdom and strength of their leaders and members. Unto all of us bestow generous and thankful hearts, ready to give and serve until the kingdoms of this world become the kingdom of our Lord and of our Christ; in whose name we have been called and pray. AMEN.

31

NONE WE DESIRE BESIDES THEE

God our Father, in whose house are many rooms and who welcomest every son and daughter who in penitence would arise from sin; in this sacred hour we would follow holy urges which beckon us unto thee. Even when we hesitate to come because of our failures and shame, thou art already meeting us to share the fullness of thy love and forgiveness. We praise thee, O God, that through the goodness which thou dost lavish upon us we are bound together as a family of grace, we hold precious things in common, we converse in the circle of prayer, and we rejoice in the house where thy honor dwelleth.

Grant unto us generous hearts which are glad when others are found of thee and receive thy bounty of grace. Make us sympathetic with those who are blinded by self-will. Help us to befriend those who grope in the misery of their disobedience. Keep us humble in the midst of our daily blessings. Let the thoughts and inspiration of this worship remind us in moments of temptation that there is none we desire besides thee.

O Lord, we number gratefully the members of our homes, friends who have been wise and true, dear ones from whom we are separated by time and space, and all for whom we covet strength and guidance. Protect them in solitary hours and give them courage for every difficulty. Let those who have heavy burdens or suffer the long strain of pain receive saving strength to endure. Comfort with a foretaste of life everlasting those who mourn.

Guide thou the leaders of our nation in love for the welfare of thy people. May thy sovereign will impress itself upon those who sit in the councils of nations, deliberating upon our destiny and that of those yet unborn. Hear our prayers for all young people. Bestow upon them bright courage and clear faith. May their lives reflect a love toward thee with heart and soul, mind and strength.

Lead us, O Holy Spirit, that in word and deed we may walk in the paths our Master trod, until we find life and joy in our eternal home; in his name. AMEN.

32

AN EVENING FELLOWSHIP OF FAITH

Everlasting God our Father, whose love the evening shadows cannot cover and whose goodness the darkness cannot hide; set thou our lives on a sure course like stars in the night. Unless thou pourest into our souls the oil of faith, our spirits are but flickering tapers along a hard path. With thy light of life, shining unto us in Jesus Christ, we can see our portion of the way and entrust the unfinished course to the brightness shining from afar. Let this worship warm our hearts, inspire our spirits, and strengthen our understanding that with new courage we may go forth as servants of the cross that redeems.

We praise thee for all who interpret the deeper meaning of life to us; for those whose faces reveal that they have been with thee, O God; for all who proclaim the gracious invitation and holy demands of the gospel; for those who leave us restless with present attainments and call us to high adventure. We thank thee for those sensitive spirits who behold thee in the unrest of the world and in every cry for bread and freedom. Above all, do we thank thee for Jesus Christ through whom thou dost come with saving judgment and with reconciling compassion.

Forgive us, dear Lord, for underestimating the power of thy Spirit in our midst, for lukewarmness in doing thy work, for failing to weigh the value of a life against the baubles of the world. O thou who seest the innermost secrets of our souls, we are ashamed that we often require of others standards of life which we do not set for ourselves. Our selfishness has often stood in the way of the progress of the gospel. Save us from the pitfalls of self-pity and pride. We would look deeply into our hearts. Convict our conscience and lead us to love and praise thee anew.

O Christ, who hast called us into one fellowship of faith; kindle our imagination and joy with the many reflections of thy light in our midst tonight. Open our minds to behold the different ways in which thy disciples have witnessed unto thee. Bind us together with thy holy church in heaven and on earth in the unity of the Spirit and in the bond of peace. Let all who yearn for a word from thee tonight hear a whisper of the Spirit. May each insight of faith and every portion of strength make us better members of thy entire body of believers so that thy kingdom may come and thy will be done; through Jesus Christ our Lord. AMEN.

THE ONE THING NEEDFUL

Father of the grace of our Lord Jesus Christ, who showest us the truly good and hast put gladness into our hearts; we adore thee for what thou art to us while we are most unworthy. Often we have forgotten the one thing needful for our life. We have searched for refreshment in the dry springs of the world's pleasures. We have withheld strength and talents from thine altar. We have failed to recognize our fellow man as thy child. Thou hast called us to be thy sons and daughters, and we have been disobedient. Appear unto us. Purge us of our sins and by thy mercy fashion us again into thy likeness.

Broaden our thoughts to think after thee; quicken our hearts to beat in smpathy for all conditions of men. Bless us with power to be creators with thee in home and in church, in work and in fellowship. Make us humble as we discover and receive thy many gifts. Bestow upon us the grace to forgive those who have wronged us and to supplant enmity with the bond of understanding.

We pray for those who face a crisis in their own life or among loved ones. Let courage and faith lead them to a victory of the Spirit. Watch over those who wait or weep; stand thou near to all who bear pain or have lost heart. Help the leaders of our nation to speak with wisdom and concern for all. Confirm the statesmen of the world in every effort toward justice and mercy. Let none be afraid to enter upon new ways which lead to lasting peace.

O God, whom we worship with one accord this holy day; make our heart thy sanctuary throughout the week. Let prayer and praise blend with our tasks. Accept our gratitude for thy healing for wounds of body and soul. Give us insight to appreciate those blessings which are ours to keep as well as those which are ours to share. Help us to prove our discipleship. Reverently we pray for the boys and girls preparing for membership in thy church. May they increase in wisdom, purity, and grace before thee and man. Strengthen every weary heart struggling for uprightness. Breathe upon every troubled soul the benediction of thy peace; through Jesus Christ our Lord. AMEN.

34

THE WALLS OF THY KINGDOM WILL RISE

Holy and ever-loving God, whose blessing and protection run beyond the feet of men; we thank thee for the glory and joy of this day. Thou foldest back the mantle of the night and revealest the lighted form of creation; take away the darkness of our souls and show us anew the image of what we were meant to be.

O God, who lookest upon the inward man; let us not be guilty of hiding what we have thought and done from thy presence. Thou seest not only our shame but our need and our faith. Fashion through thy forgiveness a new and good conscience within us. Double thou our strength with every resistance to temptation. Save us from envy and help us to use gratefully our blessings.

O Lord, we rejoice in thy church to which thou hast entrusted the good news of redemption. We acknowledge our great debt to the Christians of many nations who through their valor and faith have brought the gospel to new lands and peoples. We praise thee for the bonds of faith and fellowship which unite us with innumerable believers across earth and sea. Give us understanding minds for the oppressed and generous hearts toward the needy. When enemies of freedom and righteousness confront us, grant us endurance born out of truth. Let the whole world see that the walls of thy kingdom will rise upon the ruins of our day. Our work is of thy appointing; we ask thy guidance in doing it. O

thou omniscient God, help us all to become thy people and
to be possessed of thy saving Spirit.

We recount before thee many good things that give gladness to our lives: the faces of newborn children, joyful re-
union with those dear to us, faith on the countenances of the
suffering, healing in time of sickness, and comfort in tribulation.

Now in these quiet moments before thine altar, speak the
word of assurance we need in the heat and conflict of life.
Grant us power to do thy will amid lonely tasks through the
bond of fellowship that is in Jesus Christ our Lord; in whose
name we pray. AMEN.

35

GUARDIAN ANGELS OF THE NOBLER LIFE

God our Father, who hast created all things for a purpose
and hast touched life with beauty; open our eyes to behold
thy glory and thy wondrous will for our lives. Let not our
sins prevent us from seeking thy forgiveness. Let not our
failures close our minds to the inspiration of thy Holy Spirit.
Let not the mysteries of life keep us from comprehending
thy truths. Let not our satisfaction with present blessings
limit us in readiness to receive larger blessings. Help us, O
Lord, to search out thy reasons for blessing us so richly as
individuals and families in this church. Give us grace to
perceive that place in life where we may glorify thee.

Loving Father, we praise thee for thy renewing touch in
our lives; for thy forgiving grace in Jesus Christ; for visions
which give us holy thoughts; for inner promptings which
purify our desires; for memories which recall our vows; for
insights which keep us from foolish ways; for reminders of
thy Word, which save us in temptation; and for prayers
spoken in our behalf, which like guardian angels guide us
into nobler life.

Lord our God, make us aware as thy church that thou art yet creating a new world in which Christ reigns. Bestow upon us a humble spirit and the power of faith. O Christ, we need thy help in overcoming all hindrances to the surrender of our lives to thy love. Use us mightily in thy kingdom.

Unite us, O Spirit of Fellowship, as we intercede for the sorrowing that they may walk in thy consolation, for the sinning that they may know the Master looking upon them, for the repentant that they may hear his words "Go and sin no more," for teachers that they may see fruits ripening through the years, for workers that they may be found faithful to their trust, and for leaders that they may be followers of thine. Hear us as we bring the nameless needs of our hearts. Fashion within us a steadfast purpose, O Saviour, as we unite to serve thee in faithfulness and joy. We pray in thy holy name. AMEN.

36

THY SHEPHERDING SPIRIT

Eternal God, whose light the brightness of the day cannot comprehend and whose presence the shadows of the evening cannot hinder; we come in this holy hour to be met of thee. Touch the candles of our spirits and make them gleam with faith. Let thy Spirit, revealed so fully in our Lord's deathless life, burn away the dross of sin. Illumine us with a faith that cannot be hid.

O Christ, who art Lord of the church and dost save us into fellowship with thyself and with one another; forgive our divided witness, our lack of concern for the disinherited, and our failure to share continually thy shepherding Spirit. Make us conscious of the sacredness of thy trust to proclaim thy Word of reconciliation for our time. Let us hear the thunder of thy moral judgments. Let us feel thy love which refreshes like a gentle rain.

We rejoice that we have been called to be members of thy church. May our ties of faith fortify us against the attractions of sin and prepare us to do good. Save us from measuring attainments by standards of physical greatness or of the high praises of men. Keep us unafraid of ridicule; let thy approval make our souls leap with joy.

We praise thee for all who have prayed and labored in thy church. Grant to aged servants the reward of seeing others harvesting where they have planted. Upon those who in strength of youth are beginning their labors, bestow confidence and endurance. Empower thy servants in mission fields, in city or countryside, among the privileged or the dispossessed, until all people know thee as the Good Shepherd and become thy flock.

As each day brings us nearer our enduring home, so may each night prepare us for the rest that remaineth for thy people; through Jesus Christ our Lord. AMEN.

37

SPLENDOR OF THY SPIRIT'S INFLUENCE

O Thou, the almighty and eternal One; our hearts tremble before thee because we have so often permitted our own evil thoughts and desires to govern our lives. Thy ways are holy; purge our endeavor to limit prayer to our selfish interests. Thou art the Lord of all; pardon us for breaking life into fragments, forgetting the whole to which all belongs. Thy works are righteous; deliver us from injustice to our brother man. Thy love pleads from a cross; cleanse us of hatred and self-righteousness which quench the fires of compassion.

Merciful Redeemer, who didst lift the fallen and gavest hope where the patterns of faith had been destroyed; save us into the completeness and goodness of thy kingdom. Restore unto us the joy of thy salvation. Enthrall our souls with the silent splendor of thy Spirit's influence. Where thou art, life blossoms forever new. Come into our hearts, O God, and accept our gratitude for a life that is thine.

We acknowledge thy glory which visits the sorrowing with comfort and which through healing gives back strength of life. We praise thee for thy wisdom and care which hover around those who are facing dreaded moments and dangerous hours. We thank thee for the steadfastness of friends, the faithfulness of the consecrated, the benediction of our homes, and the guidance of thy church. Give us courage when we are fainthearted, and grant us power to resist temptation. Release us into the glorious liberty of life that belongs to thy children; through him who was obedient unto death—even Christ, our Brother and Lord. AMEN.

38

SUNDAY BEFORE LENT

O God our Father, whose love is infinite and near; place a deep unrest in our hearts until we despise evil and come to the eternal goodness for which we were made and by which we are redeemed. Lift our prayers out of petty and selfish concern. Rescue us from the emptiness of unforgiving hearts. We need a sense of holy togetherness born of thy Spirit, O living God. We have sought the best portions of life for ourselves and have forgotten that they were given also as life bread for others. Draw us to thine altar in celebration of holy things which are unseen, yet a power unto salvation. Then as we seek faith together and joy for one another, work thou in us to will and to do what is pleasing in thy sight. O Christ, fresh loveliness comes to us out of thy life as from God himself. We praise thee and give thanks for mercy that forgives, for a vision which we had lost, and for banishment of the shadow of death.

O blessed Lord, who knowest the dangers and temptations

which haunt us even when we feel ourselves to be strong; when life is kind to us, give us grateful hearts; when we falter, bestow courage; when during a portion of our days we follow thee, save us from overconfidence, lest we forget the strength which upheld us and heed not the voice which called us.

O Master of us all, we pray for those who seek release from the enslavement of sins. Come close to each one who walks the way of sorrow and solitariness. Let all who have been wounded by the cruelty of man be saved from bitterness by the kindness of a brother in Christ.

Be a strong arm unto each hand extended in the ministry of healing and restoration. Visit with thy fatherly kindness those who have lost their way as individuals, as groups, or as nations. Remove from thy church all hesitance and indifference. Fill her members with zeal to work and to bear witness in the name of him who triumphed over sin and the grave; even Jesus Christ our Lord. AMEN.

39

FIRST SUNDAY IN LENT

O God, who art perfect in righteousness yet who comest with the mercy of love to every sinner; we praise thee that in Christ thou art our Saviour. Through his suffering and death thou hast spoken to us as through none other. When the fallen were despised, he brought the forgiveness and healing of the kingdom. While he was homeless, he revealed the dwelling place of our souls. When his heart overflowed with sorrow, he brought thy comfort, O God, for the troubled in heart.

Dwell among us in this Lenten season with the Spirit that was in Christ. Make us aware that thy Word made flesh came also for us, to reveal the things that are pure and true. His holy presence disturbs our complacency and pretensions. When the Man of Sorrows sets his face toward the cross, a strange evil nature within us shrinks from his way. The temptations of the world deceive and attract us. Lord of all Gethsemanes, visit us with heavenly strength in our trials. By thy mercies, O Christ, help us to present ourselves as a living sacrifice acceptable unto thee. Let thy love which was despised and rejected of men, and which endured pain and death for our sake, triumph in us.

O God our Redeemer, let thy power revealed through the suffering and death of our Lord also cleanse and strengthen our life with our brethren. Where anger or strife invaded our homes, restore kindness and forbearance. Heal all divisions among classes and races. Bring the peoples of the earth to travel the highway of righteousness and peace. Move thy church with the spirit of the cross to lift the fallen, to guide the blind, to heal the sick, and to free those imprisoned by fear or sin. Make us unashamed of the gospel as a power unto salvation.

Inspire us to seek earnestly to follow as disciples who love thee. Help us to rejoice in the lives of the faithful who have been a benediction to us. Aid us to be a good example to our youth. In the hush of pleading hearts, let thy consolation come to the weak and bereaved until they recognize thy gracious Spirit. In good and evil hours lead us to take up our cross and to follow thee; through Jesus Christ our Lord. AMEN.

40

FIRST MIDWEEK LENTEN SERVICE— ASH WEDNESDAY

God our Father, who hast sent thine only begotten Son to bring thy saving Life to a sin-filled world; open the eyes of our souls to behold thy immeasurable love. We have no merit to plead our need. In his sacrifice thou art forever offering redemption to thy children. Guide our minds to learn of thy Christ, and incline our hearts to believe in him.

We confess that among bountiful material blessings we have often wasted and lost the gifts of the Spirit. When thy hands opened to provide food for the soul, we turned to forbidden fruit that left us hungry and ill in spirit. We have been busy about many things and have neglected the one thing needful for the salvation of our souls. We come empty, weak, and disillusioned to thee, our God, to hear the eternal story of the cross, forever new with its power to transform and bless.

O Christ, forbid that we should pass unheeding before thy cross, standing amidst each life and event of our day. With contrite hearts we come to thee in the assurance that if our sins be as scarlet, thou canst make them white as snow. Teach us then to examine our hearts, and lead us to surrender all things deceitful and unbrotherly. Take from us all contempt, envy, and covetousness. May we not grieve but love thy Holy Spirit.

O Son of God, we see thee again walking toward the cross among the believing and unbelieving, among the common people and the privileged, among the wise and the simple, and among the righteous and sinners. We behold not far from us thy lonely hours and misunderstood ministry, thy love for the outcast, and thy friendship for the forgotten. We look upon the accusations and shame which are heaped upon thy

45

love among us today. Lord Jesus, who for our sake didst face death and the bitterness of sin unafraid; enable us to see as never before the power and the glory that are thine.

Go with us, our Lord, and by patient word and searching look, through the marks of thy suffering and with a power not our own, bring us to know and to attain what we were meant to be. Bless this Lenten season that we may come to love thee above all things. In thy holy name we ask it. AMEN.

41

SECOND MIDWEEK LENTEN SERVICE

God our Father, who in Christ didst come in saving compassion to our world; give to us such faith in thee that we may know ourselves as being loved unto the uttermost. Let us feel thy deep concern for us until we shall despise the things which destroy holy gifts in our lives. Fill us with the spirit of repentance for our sins. Make us to see how they steal our happiness and undermine the foundations upon which life is built. We confess our guilt and seek thy pardon. Kindle devotion in both heart and mind, lest we make easy promises without counting the cost in effort and strength.

O Christ, thou didst lighten the burdens of humanity; teach us to bear one another's burdens and so fulfill thy law. Forbid that we should think of thy cross as distant from any of us. Lord, in thy salvation of the world is our hope; let our hope become known to all the world. Make us as a saving fellowship, a restoring body of faith, a community bearing gratefully the gift of new life that was born when thou gavest thy life for us.

Be thou gracious unto those who seek to return to thee. Encourage all who in uncertainty are searching for a sure word from thee. If some are fearful because of the greatness of their sin, then make known unto them that thou art their

Saviour also. Thy invitation is to all. Help us to find and accept thy pure forgiving love which raises us out of our shame and clothes us in the dignity of faith and the strength of grace.

Our Father, who in wisdom desirest the welfare of all thy children; inspire those who labor to perfect for peaceful use the resources and power brought to light through science. Let not the great riches and blessings of our day crucify thee afresh. Save us from the madness of vengeance and from the foolishness of impatience. Teach us that we cannot bring thee to the community and world until we have first let the love and compassion of the cross rule in our hearts. Bless thy church everywhere and make us as those who leave thee not in lonely suffering but seek to be thine in blessed companionship. In thy name we ask it. AMEN.

42

THIRD MIDWEEK LENTEN SERVICE

O God our Father, whom the night cannot hide nor evil drive away; we have come to this hour of evening prayer that in thy presence we may seek the cleansing and sanctifying light of the cross. We acknowledge that the light of our human wisdom and attainments cannot drive the darkness of sin from our hearts. We thank thee for the old and ever-new gospel of our Lord Jesus Christ. It comes to us with fresh truths and new judgments for our living. The stories of thy shame and suffering and death, O Lord, strip from us our false goodness and lead us out of our poverty of spirit to the Fountain of life.

Give us grace to welcome thy Word into our hearts. May contemplation upon the sins which led to thy crucifixion cause us to examine ourselves humbly and in repentance, O Christ. May unhallowed thoughts cease. Deliver us from the vain things which have power over us. We need the watchfulness of thy love. We must look upon thy trust as we face our own anxieties. We seek thy patience as we meet the petty round of irritations and the prosperity of the wicked. Forgive us our sins and help us by thy Spirit to walk with confidence as trusted followers for whom thou carest eternally.

We remember, dear Lord, how in the midst of the pain of body and soul thou didst care for others, even thine enemies. Give us grace to let our own discomforts or hardships bring appreciation of the needs and distress of others. Have mercy upon the sick that they may obtain faith to endure and receive strength from medicine and sleep. Let thy healing powers embrace those who are wounded in spirit or ill in mind. May the fearful have hope and courage. Teach the careless and calloused the sensitivity which remembers thee.

Arouse, O God, within thy people a zeal to bring the message of thy love in Jesus Christ to their fellow men. Let not thy church become content with present blessings or accomplishments. Lord, we are thine—may we, therefore, remain restless until everyone is found whom thou desirest in thy flock. Call us and lead us, Good Shepherd, through the gate that leads to eternal life. In thy holy name we ask it. AMEN.

43

FOURTH MIDWEEK LENTEN SERVICE

Eternal God, whose paths reach through day and night and encompass the ends of the earth, whose footsteps lead us in holy love and pursue us in fatherly mercy; we seek thee in this evening hour that in Christ thou mayest also walk beside us. Often we have run from thee in selfish pursuits, not knowing that we were removing ourselves from the dearest and best. Our feverish and uncertain pace needs the steady rhythm of things that abide. Where we have sunk in the mire of temptation and have lost our foothold on slippery promises of the world, we need to be drawn to the firm foundations of thy kingdom.

We confess that we have fashioned ways for our own selfish comfort and convenience and have called them thine. In fear and confusion we have watched thee from afar. Sometimes we have been afraid of a lonely path with thee and have chosen the road where the opinion of the crowd pleased us more than thy will. O Master of life and Redeemer of the world, we would follow anew thy leading through opposition and hatred, through trial and disgrace, through Gethsemane and Calvary, until we behold how thy way of the cross brings us the forgiveness, the life, and the victory that is in God. Walk with us, good Lord, and courage will beat in our feeble hearts. Lay thy hands upon us and joy and peace will rule our troubled spirits.

We lift up our hands in intercession for all with whom our life is bound together. We name the members of our families before thee and all with whom we tread the way of friendship. Share the boundlessness of thy mercy with the depth and length of their need until halting steps are quickened into praise and thanksgiving. Place thou the struggles and hopes of the unfortunate and oppressed peoples of the world upon our hearts. Let us not be content until we see Calvary in every anguish and in each mercy, in every sin and in each act of faith. Bless us now with those gifts which thou canst give to all as we seek the way, the truth, and the life; through Jesus Christ our Lord. AMEN.

44

FIFTH MIDWEEK LENTEN SERVICE

Infinite God, our Father, whose tender mercy is revealed for all in thy Son Jesus Christ; in the hush of this wintry night and in the peace of this holy hour there is much in our hearts which will not be still. Didst thou, Lord Jesus, watch us when in littleness of spirit we refused to share generously? Did we keep thee waiting outside the fast-closed doors of heart and mind? Did we fail to recognize thee in someone upon whom disgrace had fallen; or in a child in a distant land, hungry for bread; or in one who was looking for a kind word and a sturdy faith? In thy sight, O Lord, not one of us is justified. Before thee our hearts condemn us, yet thou art greater than our hearts. We praise thee that in thy suffering love we behold a grace which saves us.

We come to thee in faith because not our worthiness but thy goodness invites us. As we look upon thine endurance and faith throughout pain and death, we see a mercy which makes us realize that we have not loved thee nor our fellow man with our whole heart. We have complained about our small burdens when thou didst bear the sins of the world. Speak to us a word of forgiveness and create in us clean hearts and renew a right spirit within us.

God of our fathers, enlarge our faith to see how thy redeeming purpose stands above the defeats and victories of the world. To this end bless everyone who has come to the cross to find direction for his confused soul. May those who are weary and distraught receive thy peace which the world cannot give. Let none be hesitant to come to thee. May none fail to turn from evil to good and from indecision to the choice of the truth which sets life free. May the fellowship of the Spirit strengthen the weak and use the strong.

O Christ, thou who didst come to heal the hurt of the world and who didst not refuse to touch the outcasts with mercy; grant that thy compassion may dwell in us. Fortify every hand seeking to destroy prejudice, poverty, and ignorance. Impel us to spread abroad the love of God while it is day, before the night cometh and none can work any more. We ask it in the Spirit that conquered through thee, O Christ. AMEN.

45

SIXTH MIDWEEK LENTEN SERVICE

Holy Father, we thank thee for thy light and truth which lead us to thy holy hill. Reverently do we bow before thine altar in oneness of need. As we look at thy law for our life, we confess that we have broken its spirit even when we kept its outward form. Thou seest the evil inclination of our imagination. We have listened to thy Word but have not kept it in an obedient life. As we number the same sins in our life which crucified thee on Calvary, O Christ, we are ashamed of this new sorrow in thy heart. Heal us of our transgressions or we die in the midst of our living. Not until thou forgivest us with a restoring mercy can we begin life anew in thy name and with one another.

Standing before thy cross, O God, we behold the flame of thy sacrifice and reconciling love that would purify us. Grant us a repentant spirit so that we may know thy holy passion and receive the gift of thy grace. Thou who art the Son of God, light the flame of our faith and let not our love waver nor our hope falter.

As in thankfulness we name ourselves after thy Christ, O God, open before us the dimensions of our Christian calling. Make us bold to venture with thy Spirit as we speak and work. Empower us to live at peace with all men. Endue us with a long-suffering spirit, and through it bestow some quick insight of faith to all who watch us. Through gentleness make us able to enlist the interest and affection of the young. Form within us the spirit of meekness so that through patient waiting upon thee evil moods may flee. May we commend the gospel unto others because of our exceeding joy in thee.

O Lord, who didst befriend the unfortunate, the outcast and sorrowing; bestow thy gracious Spirit upon all for whom life is harsh and painful. Abide with those who endanger their lives for human safety and welfare.

Impart to the members of thy church at home and abroad the knowledge that though we have thy treasure in earthen vessels, thou wilt preserve us through him who loved us and gave himself for us; even Jesus Christ our Lord. AMEN.

46

PASSION SUNDAY

Our Father, who knowest all mysteries and lookest into the inner places of our hearts; bless our lives within that when thou comest to judge them openly, we may not be found wanting. We bring before thee the burdens of our souls, seen and unseen by human eyes: the evil thoughts which plague our imagination, the temptations which stubbornly come again when we thought them subdued, the sins against thee and our fellow man for which we cannot atone, and the guilt which we cannot lift from our conscience. O Thou to whose strength and help we never look in vain on the battlefield of our souls, give us the victory of purity and love, of courage and singleheartedness. O beautiful Saviour, let thy grace give unto our lives new joy and direction.

We praise thee, our loving and righteous God, that thou hast come to us so completely in the Christ of the cross. Let his words refresh us and his prayers set our thoughts aright. Let his anguish shame us and let his suffering reveal unto us what sin does to thee and to all. Let his endurance reveal the depth of thy love. Let his devotion in darkest hours bring out the best that is in us.

O thou eternal Spirit, present everywhere and lavishing an impartial kindness and goodness upon all as upon us; we pray for the missionaries of the cross, for the brethren in the younger churches in the world, and for all Christians under persecution. Fill them with a spirit that blesses the needy and lays low the strongholds of evil. We intercede in particular for the leaders of our nation and for the minds to whom the secret of awesome power has been given. Save us from the folly of seeking our security and peace by the threat of destruction and terror. Give us wisdom to use thy great material and spiritual energies for the good of all thy people. O thou omnipotent and all-knowing God, grant to us the open eyes of faith to trust only thee for our days and to let thine everlasting righteousness lead us out of fear into the unity and peace of thy kingdom; through Jesus Christ our Lord. AMEN.

47

PALM SUNDAY

O God, Ruler of the universe, Lord of all power, and King of our souls; we praise thee for thy Son, Jesus Christ, who brought thy reign of love and righteousness for every age. Thou openest the gates of beauty and of truth. Thanks be unto thee, O Thou who comest to enthrone the hope and spirit of thy kingdom among the multitudes of the world today.

As thou enterest the highway of our hearts, O Christ, we would welcome thee with the branches of adoration and the garments of rejoicing. Let not our devotion to thee turn into timidness and desertion when faith and justice are on trial among us. May we never spurn thine everlasting truth for the false and low standards of the crowd. Forbid that we should try to make thee our kind of king and miss becoming thy kind of followers.

O holy Conqueror of evil, as soldiers of thine make us unafraid of crosses and bravely patient in the slow victories of goodness. Establish us in true greatness of the Christian life, clothed in the stature of humility and strong in love. So may our outward loyalty to thy church be sealed by the homage of consecration, O Saviour, who hast dominion forever and ever.

O Lord, help each of us to become portals of thy entry into the lives about us. While nations shake for fear, steady us in the knowledge that thou art reigning beyond terror and tyranny. Strong Deliverer, come unto all the weary and heavy-laden and bring thy saving freedom to all in bondage of sin and under the yoke of oppression. Bring to us the peace which rises out of the triumph of forgiveness and obedience. Accept our thanksgiving for all thy servants who have been good examples unto us. May all who confirm their faith this day find joy in thy service as heirs of thy kingdom. We hail thee, thou Son of the Highest. Come to our worship and make it a coronation of life as thou, O King of Glory, enterest in. We ask it in thy name which is above every name. AMEN.

48

MAUNDY THURSDAY

God of our fathers, who in Christ hast given thy love to be our life and dost offer a Holy Supper as a memorial of thy redemption; come as a living presence into our hearts. We thank thee that in him thou hast revealed the true greatness in thy kingdom. While kings held scepters of power, thou, O Christ, didst wash the dust from thy disciples' feet. We adore thee for hallowing the humblest task and for claiming each brotherly act as a sacrament.

Thou elder Brother and divine Servant of us all, it is by thy grace that our life is reclaimed to the inner circle of thy love. Thine act of self-forgetting keeps us from forgetting

54

thee. Grant that all men may know that we are thy disciples by the love we have one to another.

O Christ our Mediator, who when alone and facing suffering didst intercede with the Father for thy disciples; may we meditate worthily upon thy prayers. We remember the strength which thou hast promised us from the Father. We remember our holy calling to declare the Father's will for this world. We acknowledge that thou wouldst have all thy followers be one as thou art one in the Father.

O Bringer of a new covenant between God and man, institute thy Holy Supper among us this night as long ago in the upper room, that it may become for us a living sign of thy saving death upon the cross. May the bread we consecrate here be the invitation for our souls to commune with the Spirit that dwelt in thy body. May the cup which we bless become the visible sign of the forgiveness and strength we receive as we partake of thy redeeming nature. May thy living presence become so real because of what we have seen by faith that through the power of thy Spirit we may be fashioned into thy likeness. We offer our supplications in thy name, whom not having seen we know and love, even Jesus Christ our Lord. AMEN.

49

GOOD FRIDAY

Merciful God our Father, on this day we behold that thou alone art good. We adore thee for thy amazing love for us in Jesus Christ. We stand in awe at the foot of the cross and perceive it as our own. With infinite compassion and divine wisdom thou hast made it thine. We come to thee though our ways are God-estranged and sin-stained. Why dost thou remember us when we have often forgotten thee, our Father? O Son from the Father's heart, why wouldst thou claim us when we often deny thy Sonship? Why dost thou continue to woo us, O Spirit of forgiveness and mercy, when we have rebelled against thy persuading? O God, in thy holy presence we acknowledge that we are thy children because of an everlasting love. O Christ, in thee we know a righteousness from God, coming not to condemn but to save us and to give itself to be our own.

We confess our pride and self-righteousness which separate us from everything we need most. We acknowledge our feeble efforts as members of thy body, O Lord. We are ashamed of our refusals to entrust our talents to thy love. We have failed to offer our strength to all who need a brotherly hand and a hope-filled spirit. We have preferred the traditions of men, the comforts of our own bodies, and the ease of undisturbed minds. Rebuke us with the grace of thy outstretched arms. Chasten us with the truth of thy holy mind. Convict us of our sins that in repentance and faith we may ask to be remembered by heaven's reconciliation. Bring our displaced emotions and desires into the Father's household of family concern. Subdue us with the suffering of thy divine heart. We would be still and know that thou art our Redeemer.

Help us this day to forgive our enemies. Give us strength to endure ridicule and hardship without losing sight of thy holy purpose for us. Make us patient while suffering innocently. Grant us grace to master bitterness and burdens, O Saviour, until they reflect faith in thy power to atone and to overcome. Let our crosses become opportunities to win a brother for thee. When we feel thee distant, our Father, grant us the trust to commend our lives into thy hands which have always blessed us. Make us thine through the grace which thou holdest forever before us on thy cross. In thy Spirit we pray. AMEN.

50

EASTER

Ever-living God, we hail thee in the risen Christ who brings to our dark world the glory of an eternal morning. Thy deathless life shines above the crosses of sin, bursts through tombs of death, and is reflected by the beauty of springtime. We would touch thee, O unseen Presence, with the hands of our doubts and behold thee with the eyes of our faith. Stir our souls with joy as thou movest among us. Let us, like Mary, hear thee calling us by name in the midst of waiting sorrow and longing loneliness. Where our heart strings have ceased to sing, let Easter's songs of victory awaken new melodies of hope. Be thou the living Master who goeth before us, healing the wounds of sin and lifting up the truth of life that would claim our love.

Lord, who hast enthroned thy grace to reign in our lives; help us to die unto sin and to live unto thee. We praise thee that thou dost dwell among us to reclaim with a forgiveness that possesses the power of resurrection and life. With thy kingdom's might link our lives with the life everlasting. Fill us as thy disciples with the strength and courage of the endless life. Save us from enslavement to things that pass away with the world. Impart unto us now in this life the throbbing joy of inseparable fellowship with thee and with all who love in thy name in heaven and on earth.

O thou who didst appear unto thy disciples when the world seemed desolate, quicken thy church everywhere with a sense of thine eternal goodness which rises anew after evil has had its empty day. Roll away the stones of unbelief and hesitancy that lie upon strong faith and bold witness. Break bread with those who have been weakened by persecution. Raise up new leaders who, like John and Peter, shall declare with breathless step thy immortal gospel. Invade thy church with the miracle of thy Spirit's life that she may be unafraid of thy cross as she seeks thy crown.

We beseech thee, O Saviour, to give some gracious sign of recognition and mercy to all whom we name in our hearts before thee. Strengthen them where ways seem hard and painful. Hallow and fulfill our imperfect hopes and prayers for them. Be merciful unto the dying. Give us anew the promise that with the final Easter dawn we shall behold an imperishable joy on the faces of all whom we have loved here and entrust to thy leading beyond the grave.

Thanks be unto thee, O God, for the victory thou hast given unto us in Jesus Christ! Keep us as thine in life and in death, and unto thee will we give our praises forevermore. AMEN.

51
SUNDAY AFTER EASTER

O eternal God, who hast shared with us thy glorious life in Christ; we thank thee for thy mystic presence, touching us tenderly yet powerfully as light caresses all growing things. Even when life's meanings are not clear, thy haunting nearness draws us to itself. Through the windows of the Spirit we gain a view of thy boundless life. Thou dost enter through closed doors of doubt and fear. Thine is a deathless communion. Thy broken body is an eternal sacrament of life and redemption which makes us whole again. Praise be unto thee, our Father.

Accompany us now on lonely and troubled ways. Make us one with others in a fellowship which reaches across the separations of sin and death. Lift our eyes beyond buried hopes and dying dreams to thy life of righteousness and love that reigneth forever. Begin with us and with thy church in making a new heaven and a new earth. Make us blessed in not having seen, yet believing thee to be the Lord of an ever-lasting kingdom.

We thank thee for all evidences of thy resurrection, O Christ: for the forces of good which are now at work in the world; for the heroism of those who fear not death nor prison in spreading thy gospel; for thy church, which is thy body of faithful and loving ones in action; for the power of truth to crush evil and to abide; for times when our hearts burn with questions; for the sharpness of thy Word which convicts our consciences; for the communion of believers in heaven and on earth; and for the vigilance of the Spirit that keeps us searching until we are found of thee.

Abide with us now, our living Redeemer, and lift our faith so that we shall not stoop to things dishonorable. Save us from murmuring against hard or monotonous duties. Illumine our spirits in the darkness of temptation and the mood of discouragement. Lead us into the way of service and steadfastness until we run with joy to find that thou dost meet each of us with the glorious power of God. We ask it in thy holy name. AMEN.

52

SECOND SUNDAY AFTER EASTER

O Lord of life, we praise thee that thou reignest in heart and home, in thy Church and in the world. We thank thee that thy goodness and mercy endure even beyond sin's crucifixion and the shadow of death. Come to our wondering, our confusion, and our ignorance, O blessed Christ, and make thy love real to each of us. Take the dimness of our souls away. Let thy comfort and thy guiding be as the sunshine on a spring morning. By the Spirit of the Father that lived so fully in thee, may thy forgiveness of our sins bring a new surge of power for fresh growth in the good life. By thy saving acts released through the resurrection for every age, come and transform our world and fill our hearts with hope.

We pray for thy Church, O God, that thou mayest fill all believers with the conviction that the gospel brings life for all. Let thy nearness inspire thy servants to boldness, diligence, and patience. May none rely on outward appearance or fleeting praise. Make us one with all believers as we hold fast to the things which endure and rejoice in having seen thee in different and wondrous ways.

O divine Companion, abide with those whose eyes are holden or whose hearts are locked. Give to those who suffer inner discord or sorrow the assurance that thou hast overcome the world. Where sickness or defeat cause spirits to grow faint, raise them with healing strength and with the fresh vigor of thy Spirit.

Now in this house of the risen Christ disclose the treasures thou holdest dear in thy kingdom. Send us forth enriched and radiant, ready to serve thee in fellowship or alone, in the consciousness that thou, O living Lord, visitest every burning heart. Unto thee be praise in thy church forevermore. AMEN.

53

GOD'S SPRINGTIME

Everlasting God, whose glory is enthroned in the heavens and touches the earth with beauty; we praise thee that thy Spirit of life and of power invades all creation and dwells in our souls. Thou hast made everything beautiful in its time and hast put eternity into our hearts. We adore thee for thy love in Jesus Christ, coming to us like the joy, the hope, and the promise of an everlasting springtime.

Arouse us out of the wintry sleep of sin and confront us with a new season of grace. Fill our souls with the influence of a Spirit, better and holier than our own, yet befriending us in our helplessness and despair. Through thy mercy our souls are again clothed with the beauty of thy goodness. Reflect upon our minds the many colors of thy truth. Change the dreary landscapes of our desires and expectations into green pastures. Hasten the growth of purity and compassion within our hearts. Lord, who art the Shepherd of our souls, lead us with all thy flock to fresh waters of strength and righteousness.

Preserve us from impatience which judges good and evil growth before the divine harvest. As the light of thy benediction falls upon the seasons of our lives, grant us love in our work, strength to bear abundant fruit, and trust to wait patiently upon thee. Let true gladness of heart increase through generous sharing of gifts in the fellowship of faith. Give grace to missionaries and leaders, and to members and pastors to sow the seed of thy Word. Help us to protect and to guide the tender growth of children. Lay upon the hearts of our young people a desire to be used of thee. Protect the weak from inward evil and outward harm. Comfort those in tribulation; guide the disappointed into new fields of fruitfulness; open embittered hearts for new blessings. Move among us as our only God; make us as those who watch and work for the coming of thy kingdom; reward us with everlasting joy and hope, for unto thee belongeth glory and majesty, dominion and power; through Jesus Christ our Lord. AMEN.

54

FESTIVAL OF THE CHRISTIAN HOME

O God our Father, who didst entrust thy Son our Saviour to the love and care of a humble family; we thank thee for thy blessings upon our homes. Thy Spirit has inspired us with power to love one another. In thy presence, O Christ, the tender bonds of life are hallowed. Thou, O God, sharest mysteries of life in the devotion of parents and children. Thou hast knit us together with the faith and sacrifice of those dear to us. Bind us as one with all families who gather around thy holy altar. Make us as citadels of faith and members of thy kingdom.

Gracious God, who providest so wondrously and wisely for us, in awe and thankfulness do we praise thee for the precious heritage of our families. Priceless treasures have flowed into our lives through the tears, laughter, and prayers of dear ones. As heirs of thine we would acknowledge that the best we have is not our own but has been given as a holy trust.

Often we have failed thee, O Giver of every good. We have disappointed those who have done much for us. Forgive our unkind words and thoughtless ways. Where we have wounded hearts that love us, stained holy vows, or shattered high expectations, grant us penitent spirits. Mold us to become worthy of the ministries and bonds of love.

O thou Head of all the families of the earth, we pray that thy name may be honored in all homes of the world. Help parents who are bowed with burdens and anxieties; shepherd the homeless children and all who are victims of cruelty and ignorance. Let a righteous anger set our hearts against every evil that violates the innocence and purity of young men and maidens. Abide with those whose loved ones suffer mental darkness. Reassure the faithful who are awaiting the glad day when forgiveness and love have their reward.

Now let our reconsecration to holy things become a blessing and a bond in thy name, that inspired, comforted, and strengthened by thy mercies, we may be found faithful in all our duties and joyful in our companionships, until at last we are called to our eternal home; through Jesus Christ our Lord. AMEN.

55

RURAL LIFE SUNDAY

O God, who art the wise Maker and gracious Sustainer of all the earth; we thank thee that thou dost entrust the seed of the field and the seed of a godly life to grow in good ground. Thy providence descends upon both the wheat and the weeds, upon the good and the evil. Thou forgettest not the mountains in their majesty nor the child in its mother's arms. As thou softenest the earth with rain, make our spirits sensitive to thy Holy Spirit; as the rays of thy sun awaken life, so stir up within us the gifts of faith; as the morning dew is distilled upon every leaf, so let this morning worship refresh our souls; as thou bringest rest with the cool of the evening, so calm our disturbed thoughts and rebellious spirits until we know thy peace.

We lift grateful hearts to thee, our Father, for all workers of the world: for those who till the soil and tend the flocks; for all who work at craft and bench, in office or in the market place; for all who toil on the sea, in mines, and in the forest; for all whose efforts provide for our comfort and security. May our dependence one upon another cause the fruits of comradeship to ripen gratefully into understanding and trust. We bless thee for all who through inventions have lightened our labors and who through heroic and patient championing of righteousness and love have united us. Join us in heart and mind that our brief lives may become a blessing upon earth.

Forgive any waste of the richness of ground and the riches of life. Teach us to conserve the treasures of stream and forest and to protect the resources of the soul. Make us good gardeners and shepherds in all our callings.

We pray for the homeless of the earth, for refugees and migrants; we intercede especially for those scattered in the strange and rough places of the world. Make our bounty a blessing to all in need and give a brotherly joy in the feeding of thy flock. Thine is the earth and its gifts! Thou hast given it into our keeping for the generations to come. When we surrender our portion of life, may it have been fruitful; and may our hearts be thankful for the miracle of thy love until we come at last to the eternal harvest where Thou wilt be our Judge and Saviour; through Jesus Christ our Lord. AMEN.

56

ASCENSION DAY OR THE SUNDAY FOLLOWING

O God, who reignest from everlasting to everlasting; we praise thee that thou camest into our world in Jesus Christ, bringing the power of love and truth to fill all things. We adore thee that his cross became a throne of redeeming love. We rejoice that as the King of life he triumphed over the dominion of death. And now we bless thee, O ascended and eternal Lord, that thou reignest forever while earthly kingdoms rise and fall. We cannot hold thee, O eternal One, with our own thoughts and traditions. Lead us to the stairway of faith, by which we seek the things which are above, that thy glory may lay hold of us here on earth.

O God, who hast exalted thy Son our Saviour after he conquered sin and death; lay the influence of thy universal Spirit upon a waiting church. Free her from worldly cares and fears of evil. Revive the power of the gospel upon the lips of parents and teachers, of ministers and missionaries. Prosper all work of thy kingdom and strip us of selfish concerns which hinder the unity of thy Church universal. We bless thee for insights into things unseen and eternal, and for the bond of holy fellowship with the company of the faithful in heaven and on earth.

Make haste to save the nations of the earth, lest through

the folly of war and the fear of distrust we destroy homes, cities, and lands. With the scepter of thy mercy and wisdom turn us from discord, strife, and division. Replace all contempt for others in our hearts with prayers for their salvation. Take from us all boasting and self-righteousness and make us to see that none can rise before thee without lifting a brother. With thee is our hope, in thee is our trust, and from thee shall come our comfort and peace.

O God, who art all-knowing; enable us to come to thee freely in this hour of holy elevation, for thou art close to every weakness and to every holy desire. Let the troubled in mind find thy thoughts, let the sorrowing discover the doors of heaven, and may the hesitant receive a steadfast faith. Grant that we may praise thee through consecrated lives until thou dost lift us out of mortality into the joy and glory everlasting; through Jesus Christ our Lord, who reigneth with thee and the Holy Spirit forever. AMEN.

57

PENTECOST

Almighty God our Father, who dost create and inspire all that has breath of life; we adore thee as thy Spirit draws us together in wonder and praise. O gracious Spirit that dwelt in Christ, touch our spirit that we may know ourselves as children of God. Incline our hearts to repentance and humility that in fruitful waiting of faith new life may abound.

Spirit of the goodness of God, breathe upon us the gifts of joy and peace, until we throb with a sense of thy nearness. Kindle the fire of love within our hearts, until we can no longer hold its warmth to ourselves alone. Heal us of fear and disunity in our witnessing for the gospel. Light the flames of holy understanding that we may know truth and salvation as the language thou dost speak to all. Let thy Word thunder and whisper thy will for our time. Baptize us with the unity of the Spirit and the bond of peace. Form in us anew the mind of Christ that we may follow thy call as joyously and bravely today as the apostles, martyrs, and saints of every age.

Spirit of Christ, who art our Life and Guide; we pray for the health and strength of thy church. Let us not be afraid to express the life whereby we are saved. Keep our hearts from forgetting those to whom thou wouldst minister. With the liberty of the Spirit free us from outworn traditions, useless form, and pious insincerity. Take the blindness of our souls away and restore the vision of a triumphant fellowship in which every race and people shall acknowledge thee as Lord.

Spirit of intercession, bind us with all members, teachers, and servants of thy Word. Surround them with power and bless unto them our interest and gifts. Raise up many leaders and servants of zeal and stature among our young people.

O calm Strength of the Spirit, lift us out of discouragement and self-despising. O comforting Presence of Christ, minister unto all the bereaved and afflicted. O Spirit of peace, take away the bitterness of our hearts and let thy refreshing streams bring forgiveness and new beginnings in young and old. O Spirit of God in Christ, who wast, art now, and art to come, lead us through peril and temptation, in life and in death, and reign within us forevermore. AMEN.

58

AFTER PENTECOST

O God our Father, who dost share with all mankind thy Spirit which lived so fully in Jesus Christ; we praise thee for every stirring of thine within our souls. Thy Spirit does not leave us satisfied in a life of sin; we thank thee for awakening our consciences. Thou dost not leave us to ourselves; we rejoice in the deep yearnings calling us home to thee. Thou dost not let us rest with present attainments; we are grateful for the more excellent way of love. Thou dost not leave us weak and helpless; we adore thee for a Spirit which comforts, saves, and leads us into Christ's truth and life.

In this glad worship we are mindful that thou wouldst increase and fulfill every individual blessing through fellowship with others. Grant us, good Lord, thy forgiveness as we confess our divisions, our looking away from the needs of others, and our desire to be thy favorite children when ours is a church for all the world. Touch us with thy Spirit's breath and flame. Bestow upon each of us the awareness that thou wouldst save us into a holy togetherness, to love and serve in thy world-wide Church.

Empower thou the work of Christian missions. Grant to all ministers and members in our mission churches the courage, faith, and resources necessary to establish new fields. May thy Spirit stir us to live worthily as members of thy church, to give in thy name, and to dare for thy truth.

We implore thee to look mercifully upon the needs of all who wait for thy Spirit's healing in sickness, sorrow, or distress. Give them and us faith to trust thy abundant mercies.

Keep us faithful unto the end and finally bring us to everlasting life; through Jesus Christ our Lord, who with thee and the same Spirit liveth and reigneth, one God, world without end. AMEN.

59

THE FRUITS OF THE SPIRIT

Everlasting God, whose Spirit brought the life and order of creation into the world; brood over our unruly spirits until they reflect thy divine image. In Christ we behold the fullness of life for which our spirits hunger. Move among us and within us, O Spirit of God, that we may receive thy power and glory in our lives. Increase the fruits of the Spirit in us until all thoughts and desires become obedient unto the mind of Christ.

Fill us with the *love* of Christ, which seeks not its own but suffereth long to win a brother.

Grant us *joy* in doing thy will and in the knowledge that we are thine.

Give us *peace* the world cannot give and which is the flower of forgiveness and trust.

Grant us *patience* until we fret not over evil but wait upon thee to establish the ways of righteousness.

Bless us with *kindness* that hearts may seek thy face.

Strengthen us in *goodness* that we may commend the gospel and serve as thy sons and daughters.

Bestow upon us *gentleness* that the sorrowing may be comforted and tender ones may be drawn unto thee.

Guide us in *faithfulness* that our gratitude to thee may be known and we may inherit eternal life.

Empower us with *self-control* to rule our own spirits and to become fit instruments for thy will.

O God, the Father, the Son, and the Holy Spirit; send power from on high to establish thy Church and to bring honor to thy kingdom. So may we minister in thy name and witness to the Life that would fashion us into a new creation; for the sake of him who died and rose again and ever liveth to make intercession for us, even Christ our Lord. Amen.

60

ORDINATION

O God our Father, who hast made us to be thy children, whose love in Christ is our life, and whose Spirit inspires our faith; we praise thee for all thy goodness and mercy which have followed us all our days. Praise be unto thee for all who have kept the fellowship of the Spirit and whose example, prayer, and work have established the church in our midst.

We thank thee that today we may behold the fruit of thy mercies being shown from generation to generation! For Christian homes and parents, who implanted the first roots of faith, for pastors and teachers who nurtured the flowers of character and trust, for singers of hope and brave cross-bearers, for all who comforted and counseled us with the eternal kindness and truth, for the godly heritage of thy church which welcomed us when we were born and led us to thy holy altar, we give thee our thanks. Humbly do we adore thee as we behold a great cloud of witnesses urging us to lay aside every weight and sin that would hinder in the great race before us. We are not worthy of thy boundless gifts of love and sacrifice, and need also the gift of forgiveness and grace to stand in their succession.

And now, O Christ, who callest each of us to follow thee into the kingdom of God; we pray for thy servant who presents himself for consecration to the Christian ministry. Let thy Spirit dwell in him so that he may preach thy unsearchable riches. Give him the grace to lay thy claim upon many hearts. Let courage, wisdom, and compassion mingle with his shepherding of souls. May he daily handle sacred things with reverence and touch life as belonging unto thee. Give to all of us the holy joy that has come to him and to his loved ones. We marvel at thy wondrous work and blessing in each life and family in our church.

Thou great and good Shepherd of thy flock, grant to us and to all ministers, missionaries, and members of thy church the grace to see all days as in thy sight, to love not only those who love us but all for whom thou carest, to carry any cross placed upon us with strength from thy cross, to translate the riches of this world into treasures of thy kingdom, to count all things loss for thy sake, and to serve thee in single obedience that there may be one flock and one Shepherd in thy church.

Our Father, who hast ordained us to a royal priesthood that each may pray to thee and for one another; remember with thy favor and power all who are champions of righteousness, all people who are waiting for a word of redemption for body and soul, the servants of the cross in distant lands and here at home, the teachers in our seminaries and colleges, and every young person listening for thy call in his or her life.

Having dwelt on the mountain of vision and prayer, may we come to the valley of human sorrow and need, bringing a ministry of reconciliation and peace which the world cannot give but by which it is saved unto eternal life; through Jesus Christ our Lord. AMEN.

61

MEMORIAL DAY

O God, eternal Ruler of all peoples, who art terrible in thy judgments and swift in mercy, whose Spirit broods over the clash of swords and the still sleep of the dead; hallow thou our memories of the heroes and victims of war. Let the Spirit of Christ resurrect within us the things which make for our peace. Humbly and gratefully do we acknowledge the many blessings of our land, nurtured not only by sunshine and rain but by heroism and sacrifice unto death. Forgive us for having taken the gifts of our heritage as if we deserved them. Reverently we would take broken dreams from the hands of the fallen, to live again by thy grace in us. Our life is bounded by the full measure of devotion of those for whom life, even as our own, was filled with sweet hope and high visions. Let us then not handle lightly the dreams of brother hearts nor deal carelessly with freedom born in blood and sorrow.

Lord of the hosts of the dead and Redeemer of the living,

rebuke all vainglory and all lust for land or wealth which blind us to thy fatherhood. Save us from a vindictive spirit and harshness of heart that hinder good will and comradeship in Christ's name. Lead us from the many strange altars of power and war to thy holy presence. There may we know the way of salvation for all mankind. Make us strong and brave to carry the light of freedom and truth in this time of grace.

O God, who givest comfort and cheer to the lowly and the waiting; we intercede for all whom war has cursed with suffering: the sick and the maimed, those who sit in mental darkness and terror of the past, those who look in vain for the return of loved ones, and those who are shelterless and hungry. Bind us together into a beloved community of compassion until we find thy restoring mercies and the fruits of love and justice.

Our Father, whom the darkness of hate and strife cannot overcome; reveal thyself in Jesus Christ as the Ruler who can make all things new. Make us ready to pay the cost of striving for a world-wide family of nations. Implant within the hearts of all leaders the divine passion to uplift the weak, to free the oppressed, and to share thy bounty. Let all messengers of the gospel be as the wings of peace. So teach us to look through tears and hopes unto thy kingdom in which none who believe in thee shall die and all shall live in everlasting righteousness and peace; through Jesus Christ our Lord. AMEN.

62

FESTIVAL OF THE HOLY TRINITY

O triune God, Creator of the heavens and the earth, who dwellest in light unapproachable; glory be unto thee, for thou art our Father and hast made us to be thy children.

Thou whose holiness would consume all evil, we rejoice in thy love and salvation which have blessed us in Jesus Christ. O Spirit of the Father, living and reigning from all eternity and dwelling completely in the Son, our Saviour, we adore thee for thy gift of wisdom and power unto every believing heart. Our Father, though our minds cannot comprehend the mystery and wonder of thy ways, yet thou art the one true God who is our Life, our Love, and our Light.

Inspire us to worship thee in singleness of heart. Unite us with thy will for all mankind so that we may go and make disciples of all nations and baptize them in thy name. Fill us with thy love and form us into one body of faith on earth and in heaven.

Ever-living God, take from our minds all small thoughts which are as graven images of thee. Save us from selfish prayers and presumptuous ways. We would be reverent before thy holy presence; we stand in wonder before thy infinite thoughts; we owe our lives to thy boundless grace. Through divine mercy forgive our littleness of faith, our foolish fears, our proud ways. Open unto us thy unsearchable riches in Jesus Christ. Meet us with a vision of thy kingdom of righteousness and truth.

O God, who withholdest no good thing; teach us to use our smallest and greatest gifts as in thy sight. In our needs and in our sorrows guide us to the springs of eternal strength. Kindle with holy fire the hearts of all who teach and learn, who lead and follow, and who work and wait. Bring thy church into true communion with thee, O Lord of life and love. Make us one with all who wrought mightily and bore patiently in thy name. Praise be unto thee, Father, Son, and Holy Sipirit, one God, to whom belongeth honor and dominion, power and glory forever. AMEN.

63

SOUL OF OUR SOULS

Everlasting God, our small minds cannot reach the beginning nor the end of thy thoughts, but thou art always thinking of us, thy children. Thou art infinite in majesty and art yet the intimate joy of our spirits. We worship and adore thee, mighty God, the Father of our Lord Jesus Christ. How beautiful is thy holiness, O Soul of our souls! How awesome are thy judgments; how tender is thy mercy!

The world is too much for us until we come into thy sanctuary, O Lord. Here we are bound together in the faith of thy holy Church. Here we remember all who have labored and sacrificed that we may live. Here we learn a truth that is timeless. It is brought to us by a Spirit which teaches, reproves, and loves us.

We name before thee the sins within, not seen by human eyes. Free us from empty outward charm which covers poverty of soul. Replace our unforgiving spirit with greatheartedness. Remove from us the stubborn mind that refuses to believe the wonder of thy presence. Aid us to see the glory that is hidden in the lives around us. Form us to become vigorous members of the body of faith.

Our Father, give us grace this week to widen our interest in the spiritual welfare of humanity. We remember thee, Lord Jesus, among the outcast, the unwanted, and the distressed. Let not our own prosperity or security make us insensitive to the misery and hopes of the unfortunate.

Bestow thy compassion upon minds that are sick and disturbed. Guard them from terror by night and from dark imaginings by day. Entrust knowledge and resources of healing to all who minister with medicine and counsel.

We intercede for all who are harassed by disagreement or

enmity. Lead them out of bitterness and revenge, which blight the innocent and guilty alike. Bless them with the reconciliation that comes to open hearts and minds. Set thou a banquet of joy and thanksgiving for them. Not of our worthiness, but of thy tender mercy that was in Jesus Christ, hear our prayer. AMEN.

64

THY WORD WEARING THE FLESH OF HUMANITY

God our Father, in whose presence we feel the hush of eternity, whose Word we heard in Jesus Christ wearing the flesh of humanity, and through whose Spirit thy voice speaks to every heart; we adore thee for placing a fellowship of love and faith in our keeping. If we were to leave thee, we should forsake all that inspires, all that brings hope, and all that reveals a plan for our living. With thee there is strength other than our own, and we meet a love that is faithful beyond a cross. Thy mercy ministers to rebuild our shattered purposes lying in ashes. In thee we see our fellow man as a brother for whom Christ has died. We praise thee, our Father, for thy amazing love declared unto us in the gospel.

While thou hast been so immeasurably gracious toward us, O God, we must confess that we have not loved thee with all our heart and mind and soul and strength. We have not loved our neighbor as ourselves. We have sought to bend thy law to our own devices. We have appropriated gifts intended for thy family of faith, as if they were ours alone. Thou knowest our frame and rememberest that we are dust. Soften our hearts with contrition and join our hands in reconciliation. Teach us to look upon our own faults and weaknesses and not upon those of others. Free us from our unfounded fears. Cleanse us of every wicked desire and intent. Give us pure hearts that we may see thee again, O holy and forgiving God.

We remember thy church in all lands, O Christ, where thy followers worship in secret or under oppression. Raise up there and here alike leaders of vision and perseverance. Uphold those who care for the sick and needy, the aged and helpless. Deliver those who live in the prison house of evil habits and guide them into the joyous freedom of an obedient life. Lay thy hands upon all whose welfare is precious in our sight.

We lift our eyes unto quiet hills and still streams, to be strengthened and refreshed in spirit. Having tasted thy goodness, O Son of the living God, lead us into paths of righteousness for thy name's sake. AMEN.

65

OUTDOOR SERVICE

Eternal Father, whose face no man has seen; we praise thee for thy glory which meets us each day. Thy beauty is upon us, in lakes and fields, among rivers and mountains, in song and worship. Thy fairest likeness and glory are not of this earth but of thy goodness, walking with us in thy Son, our Saviour Jesus Christ. In him we behold the wonder of thy love.

We bless thee, O God, for thy holy laws, thy marvelous power, and thy gracious providence by which our lives are sustained. We stand in awe before thy ways, known and unknown, which dawn with the morning and subside not in the quiet of the night. Our spirits are hushed, for by the testimony of faith and the discoveries of wise men we can trace thy footprints. By the whispering of thy Spirit, wooing our better selves, we know that thou art near. Forgive our dullness of heart when burning bushes beside our path leave us unmoved, when joyful faces of little children do not recall for us the nature of thy kingdom. Forgive us that our busyness and anxiety rob us of thy quietness and confidence for our souls, that we so often separate physical beauty and wealth from the beauty and riches of the Spirit. Forgive us that we have not seen the ugliness of sin nor the grace of the good life, that we have often failed to love one another in the name of him who would weave our lives together with the splendor of a kingdom that fadeth not away. O thou unwearied God, who dost never fail us; let us not fail thee. Help us to hold our many blessings as a shield against temptation; help us to gather the strength of joy for hard tasks.

We pray for all who are in prison, for all who suffer the consequences of wrong choices. Guide them in new ways and cause our sympathy to help in their condition. Visit with thy healing Spirit the sick and distressed. Let the light of Thy countenance stream upon those who are sightless or sit in darkness of soul and mind.

In the hush of these moments of prayer direct thy Spirit to unite us as a church with Christians throughout the world that their prayer and work may become our own and thy gospel may unite us in one faith and calling.

Teach us now, Lord Christ, how to listen and how to rest, how to labor and how to trust thee for reward, until at last we behold thee in everlasting glory and love; unto whom belongeth praise forevermore. AMEN.

66

INDEPENDENCE DAY

Almighty and everlasting God, who in wisdom hast established our nation through the faith and devotion of our fathers; we praise thee for the gracious guidance and bountiful providence with which thou hast prospered each generation. Through peril and storm thou hast led us with the light of truth to the rock of liberty. Mercifully thou hast recalled us from error, division, and strife to holy ways of freedom. Make us to be good stewards of all thy mercies for a blessing in all the earth.

O thou Sovereign-Creator, we rejoice in the beauty, fertility, and strength which flow from rugged mountains and through slumbering valleys, in the treasures of the earth and over fair plains, on winding rivers and in the stillness of lakes. Thy benediction descends upon giant cities, humble villages, and solitary homes. We adore thee for the good things thou hidest in the hands of the mighty and the lowly. Teach us to use all power in reverence and with integrity.

Thou who givest strength for the rising of nations, righteousness for their endurance, and judgments that evil perish and good be enthroned; embrace us and all mankind with thy love in Jesus Christ. Cleanse our hearts of prejudice and greed. Preserve us from corruption in industry and in government. Save us from deceit in our schools and homes. Fashion us as clean, strong instruments in thy hands. Make our consciences alert to a holy Will for all people.

O God, without whom no nation can dwell securely; arm us with the weapons of the Spirit to fight falsehood with truth and half-gods with living faith. Keep us from contentment that stifles the voice of duty. Arouse us from ease which is deaf to the cries of the poor, the homeless, and the downtrodden. Give us a brotherly heart.

O God, out of whose fatherly hand have come the races of man; aid us to treasure every godly heritage brought to these shores. Send us on new and holy errands for truth and brotherhood. Fortify us and all our leaders with a vision of peace and with a zeal for righteousness. Let thy Light lead us to be a land of hope and promise for all who trust in thee; through Jesus Christ our Lord. AMEN.

SEND US INTO THE WORLD

Eternal God our Father, who hast formed all hearts to love thee; we thank thee that through Jesus Christ the glory of thy love fills every heart that hungers after righteousness. Thou makest all ways lead to thee! Praise be unto thee, O divine Companion, walking beside our faltering steps. We thank thee for all thy servants of every time and place, who have journeyed by faith and have worked mightily in thy kingdom. We are grateful for all Christian lives, which like stars have lighted lonely and desolate places. Why hast thou blest us so wondrously if it be not to know and love thee, O God?

We come as thy children to be claimed of thee, as members one of another to be inspired of thee, as those who have failed thee and our fellow man to be restored by thee. Thou knowest the sins which beset us most. Forgive us with the love by which Christ gave himself for the church. Keep our hearts from hatred, our minds from evil, and our speech from guile. Remove all that separates us from faith and love in thy name. Renew our calling as fellow workers of thine. Send us into the world as disciples of thy beloved Son who came that all who hear and believe may have eternal life.

Save thy children from the cruelties of war, and lead the nations in the way of peace. When the world offers false pleasures and riches, teach us that there is no wealth except life in thy kingdom. Have compassion upon broken hearts and heal them. Remember the fallen and raise them. Have mercy upon all deluded minds and illumine them. Have pity upon the ignorant and enlighten them.

Bestow upon us such humility in spirit, such purity of life, and such strength of purpose that in the days before us we may be good instruments in the hands of truth and love.

Grant that through the din of earthly interests and through the storm of human passion the voice of thy Spirit may be heard and many hearts may be persuaded for thy kingdom. In thy holy name we pray. AMEN.

68

A FOREGLEAM OF THE SPLENDOR

God our Father, who art the Giver of all good, who sustainest all life, and who clothest all things with wisdom and beauty; we give thanks for thy faithfulness from one generation to another. We come here as did our fathers and mothers, mindful that thou openest thy hands to satisfy the desire of every living thing.

We are grateful, O Lord, that to the laughing eyes of little children thou dost bring joy, to the searching eyes of youth thou revealest the wonder and order of the universe, to the discerning eyes of the mature thou dost disclose thy glorious truths clothed in mystery and faith, and to the dim eyes of the aged thou dost grant vision to see the beauty of this world as a foregleam of the splendor of life that endureth forever.

As thou dost gather us in prayer to become more like thy people, we give thee our heartfelt gratitude for our Saviour, Jesus Christ. Thou not only art the Creator of the world, but in him thy power to redeem comes unto us.

Touch us with thy Spirit so that the roots of evil may be cut off within us. Heal the wounds of sin and help us to grow and increase abundantly in the summertime of our soul. Bless our congregation so that thy life-giving Spirit of the gospel may bear the fruit of Christian living. Open our ears to hear thy servant witness to the hope and strength that comes from thee.

Our hearts remain hushed as all creation whispers a psalm

of praise. Be thou, O loving Spirit, especially near to those who find the glory of nature removed from them.

O Spirit of the everlasting God, who alone canst bring light out of darkness; grant peace in our time and make us to be thine in obedience and love; through Jesus Christ our Lord. AMEN.

69

THE UNSEARCHABLE RICHES

O God our Father, good beyond all that is good, fair beyond all that is fair, in whom is our peace; reveal unto each of us the unsearchable riches in Christ. Show us, ere our life is spent, our poverty of soul when only riches of the world are our possessions. Take from us all impurity and blindness of heart that we may own thy love and behold the treasures in life.

Searcher of hearts, whom none can deceive and who deceivest none; we confess that we have been slow to perceive thy immeasurable goodness toward us. We have not entered the open doors which lead to eternal life. We have loved the deceptions and distortions of temporal things which bring no answer to the questions which haunt our brief stay on earth. Impart to us the greater joys and rewards which belong to thy kingdom. May we see them as a pearl of great price and surrender all lesser possessions. We would seek for that which abides when friends forsake us and afflictions assail. We seek for that which is more precious than fine gold or more dear than the desires of our bodies.

O God, our empty hands and pleading hearts are testimony to the grace by which we live. Find us, our Father, in our seeking and be thou the fulfillment of our deepest hungers. We adore thee for the riches of the Spirit that were in Jesus Christ; in thy forgiving mercy we receive divine strength; in thy healing power we receive the health of our spirits; in thy Word we know the truth that sets us free; in thy love we find the true meaning for our living; in thy church we are invited into the fellowship of the kingdom; in thy risen Life we know an imperishable hope and joy. May we find gladness not in what may be called our own, but in what we may share in thy name. Strengthen our missionaries and teachers everywhere until the springs of the Spirit appear in the wilderness.

Unto thee do we commit ourselves and all who are one with us, praying that nothing may separate us from thy love which is in Christ Jesus our Lord. In whose name we pray. AMEN.

70

THE ABIDING REFUGE

Holy and eternal God, out of the storms of the world we come into this quiet place to worship thee who art the abiding Refuge. Thanks be unto thee for silence which unfolds strength and for tranquillity leading us to things deep and true. Meet with us here in the inner place of our spirits and refresh us with thy living presence.

O God our Father, who hast made all things for man and man for thy glory; sanctify our bodies, minds, and souls, making us willing servants of Jesus Christ. Let our approach to thee be of the heart and not of the lips only. Let us meet thy unspeakable mercies and gifts of love with humility, obedience, and thankfulness. In the clatter of the world we often do not hear the still, sad yearnings of suffering humanity; thinking of our needs, we find it easy to forget that every need in the world is our neighbor in Christ. Build our lives into a thoroughfare of mercy and of understanding.

O Spirit of God, touch our lives with thy power and serenity that we may resist evil and with confidence champion the gospel. Through communion with thee let us be aware of thy renewing and inspiring goodness which is as constant as the heavens above us. Free us from old irritations and small comparisons. Give power to our faint hearts to accept tasks wholeheartedly in thy name. Release our courage from fear and suppressed anxieties. Hallow our passions and our strength through consciousness of thy holy guiding.

O Love eternal, in thy good time prosper and strengthen us in the work we have undertaken in thy name in family, church, and commuity. May the world not mold us today; make thou us strong enough to mold the world. O God, we must give an account of each day of our life when the night cometh. Keep us then watchful and true by fastening our eyes upon thee who didst endure the cross for the joy set before thee. By thy grace make us partakers of this thy joy, O blessed Redeemer. Continue to call us to be thy disciples until in serving thee we find perfect freedom. In thy name we ask it. Amen.

71

SUMMERTIME

O everlasting God, whose living Spirit has brought all things into being; we glory in the wonder of thy creation. Thy mind has given order to the universe; we bless thee for thy truths and laws, often hidden in unfathomable ways. Thou hast revealed thy love in Jesus Christ; we praise thee for thy immeasurable goodness in thy continual redemption. We come to thee, our Father, needing thy guidance and sustaining, thy judgment and comfort.

Thou who hast fearfully and wondrously made all things, direct the eyes of our understanding to see the work of thy hands in the beauty, form, and bounty of nature. Since all mysteries and knowledge have been known to thee from the beginning of the world, inspire us with a reverent spirit as we discover and explore. Make us mindful that children and flowers, stars and atoms, and all that hath life and form were fashioned as good in thy sight.

Holy God, who dost place each generation of men into a new garden of blessings and freedom; forgive us for our self-will and disobedience in the use of thy gifts. While fruit-laden boughs reflect thy lovingkindness, we have often wasted or withheld food while many hungered. Cleanse and restore the image of thyself within us. Make us as thy children, bound together with all who seek to know thy will for all the earth.

O Christ, who didst speak at mountainside and field; grant us a new awareness of thy presence as the summer's majesty and splendor, rest and gladness, surround us. Give to those who are filled with anxieties for tomorrow sufficient strength for today. Keep us from evading tasks with useless dreaming. Guide us in work, play, and companionship into ways which cause us to return to thine altar with joy and thankfulness. Lead the heavy-laden by thy Spirit into green pastures and refreshing streams. Grant grace unto us and to thy church everywhere to declare the gospel of thy glorious life and kingdom. So may men know and believe that thou art Lord and Redeemer of all, to the glory of the Father; in whose name we pray. AMEN.

72

THY TIMELESS HEARTBEAT
NEAR OUR HEART

O God, who in fatherly wisdom hast given us freedom to lock or unlock our heart's door; teach us the secret of an open heart. Let our waiting for thy knock become a reverent desire to please thee as loving children. When words fail us and our thoughts are barren, teach us to be still and know that thou art all in all. If our soul's image of thee is uncertain, put thine arm around us. May we feel the strength of thy majesty and the reassurance of redeeming love.

O Spirit of the Eternal, at times we find it easy to commune with thee. When beauty and joy flood our life, and thou providest in abundance our creature comforts, we are thankful. When life is healthy and strong and our efforts meet with success, let us not fail to see the deeper meaning in thy blessings for us. Save us then from pride and make our life a song of praise.

Lord of mystery and holiness, often we find it hard to commune with thee. In mercy and patience bend thou close to the mists of uncertainty until we recognize that it is the Lord. When we are overwhelmed by our weakness and failure, come to us as a Friend of sinners. If we feel no need of prayer, reveal thy fingerprints upon every gift and the marks of Christ's sufferings upon the world's sorrows and broken hopes. When we seek thy face and remember grievances which keep a brother or sister from thy altar and fellowship, show us the way of reconciliation. When anxieties press in to suffocate the breath of the Spirit, give us faith to breathe deeply the winds of heaven's promises. When burdens oppress us, be thou like a shadow of a mighty rock in the heat of the desert. If any of us are beset by doubt, then let us reach out in mind and spirit until we feel thy timeless heartbeat near our hearts. Let us not be afraid to follow the reasoning of faith when it outreaches the reasoning of our minds. May radiance upon our faces be the sign that we have been with thee; through Jesus Christ our Lord. AMEN.

73

10/18/59

WONDROUS ARE THY WORKS!

O God, whose splendor is revealed in all creation; we call to remembrance thy faithfulness and lovingkindness toward

84

us and the world in which we live. We praise thee for the order and constancy of nature, for the beauty of earth and sea and racing cloud, and for the bounty of the fruitful fields. We thank thee, our Father, that thou hast given us the warmth of human fellowship and the love of those intimately dear, our home blessings and the pure pleasures of life as we rejoice in thee and in one another. We are grateful for the trustfulness of little children, for the weak who need us, and for the strong who give us of their strength.

Thou dost bless us with the joy of work, the zest of sport, the breath of the wind and the warmth of the sun upon our faces. Thou dost gladden our hearts with the wild things in forest and stream. Wondrous are thy works, O God!

But above all do we praise thee for thy love and righteousness which have shined in the face of Jesus Christ. In him, fairer than all nature, we behold thy meaning for all of life. In him all voices of nature join in a glorious song of redemption.

Father, who hast blessed us with so many provisions in seedtime and harvest; give us the grace to be one with those who must remain in rooms of sickness or are held by unfortunate circumstances. Make us aware of the thousands who are starving because of ignorance and superstition or because of the horrors of man's destruction. Forgive us where we have tolerated filth and disease and overcrowded conditions to exist in our cities, when thou desirest to fill the earth and every life with beauty and strength. As each flower and waving branch is called to bear fruit in its due season, so may our lives follow thy will in Jesus Christ and know that the glory of nature and the glory of redemption are all Thine.

O Lord, grant us the forgiveness of our sins and give us strength, that having praised thee with our lips, we may also praise thee in consecrated and faithful lives; through Jesus Christ our Lord. AMEN.

74

LABOR DAY

O God our Father, whose name is excellent in all the earth and who hast made man to have dominion over the work of thy hands; we offer thee our thanksgiving for every task and gift in our keeping. We rejoice that through Christ thou callest us all into comradeship with thyself. Gratefully do we acknowledge the gift of mind with which to plan and dream, the gift of hands with which to fashion and toil, and above all the gift of soul in which to reflect thy image.

O Thou who workest in perfect justice and love, forgive us for having coveted a fellow man's gain or blessing. Forbid that we should seek easy profit without remembering that we are our brother's keeper. Cleanse us of our sins and give us grace to plan and work for others as we would have them do for us.

O Christ, whose hands knew both toil and agony and were extended with blessings from the Father; inspire us to work and worship together as we seek bread and joy for body and spirit. Teach us to think not only upon each other's demands but also upon the highest hopes and prayers. As each laborer is worthy of his hire, so may each give his efforts in full measure. Cause righteousness to flow like a mighty stream in country and city that we may glorify thee in every relationship.

O God, who hast bound us together in this bundle of life; help us to repay our benefits to those who bear heavy responsibilities, to those who labor for our protection and stand in much danger and temptation, to the aged who deserve rest from their labors, to those who have been injured or crippled in dutiful work. Befriend and strengthen all who face monotony and great weariness. Have mercy upon those who are embittered by misfortune or injustice. Give us a deep concern for all who are unemployed.

As we pray together in this Christian church, coming from all walks of life and bringing many needs and perplexities, grant us inward renewal and the bond of Christian fellowship. Prepare us to return to our office or factory, our home or shop, ready to labor together not for the things that perish but for the glorious life in thy eternal kingdom; through Christ our living Lord. AMEN.

75

THY RECONCILING FELLOWSHIP

Eternal God, whose light and truth shine through the face of Jesus Christ into the shadows and darkness of our world; we lift up our eyes in faith to thee. We need a new vision of a kingdom which endures, while earthly kingdoms rise and fall. We need to behold the saving Life and Spirit of the Lord of the church while vain and temporal things tempt her love. Let the good news of the gospel shine clearly while evil forces threaten her life. Speak to us thy living Word with its redeeming power, rebuking our sin and working in us the miracle of cleansing.

Father, we thank thee for all the heroes, martyrs, and servants of the faith who have boldly declared thy truth, who have ministered in love, and who have sealed their testimony with their blood. Let their lives and sacrifices turn our lukewarmness into untiring devotion. Empower all ministers, teachers, and parents with thy Spirit. Let hope, wisdom, and prophecy be born in our schools and seminaries.

Let thy church become as her Lord, a lowly servant, ministering to the woes, the sickness, and the hunger of humanity. Enable thy prophets to speak without fear and give us courage to follow them. Let the secret influence of thy Spirit fortify us against love of ease and fear of ridicule. Send with each task the strength that keeps us faithful.

Comfort the sorrowing and uphold those who waver in trust. Where conscientious effort seems to bring no reward, give a word of reassurance that it was done unto thee. Sustain all evangelists and missionaries, all who are persecuted, and those whose testimony is received with joy.

O Christ, who hast given to us one faith, one life, and one kingdom; woo us in the midst of our divisions and suspicions into thy reconciling fellowship, that we, as followers of thine, may all be one in thy name. Let thy glorious life move through all creed and doctrine, all forms and institutions, to fashion a church that is without spot, wrinkle, or blemish, ready to bear the fruits of the Spirit. To this end bless thou the world-wide fellowship within thy Church. Hasten the day, O God, when the kingdoms of the world shall become the kingdom of our Lord; in whose name we pray. AMEN.

76

FOR DISCIPLESHIP

Our Father, who in Christ hast come into the world as a saving Servant and who callest us to be disciples in his name; we praise thee for the glorious company of apostles, martyrs, and witnesses who carried the gospel beyond their own borders into all nations. O God, we are breathless with wonder as we behold thy life in Jesus Christ. Still thou art going before us in everlasting truth and leadest us with the power of thy eternal Spirit. Yet thou dost patiently wait for us when we linger behind—confused, blinded, and leaderless. When we stumble in our sins, thou dost raise us to the stature of righteousness. When in overconfidence we venture beyond our wisdom and strength, thou lookest upon us as an understanding Friend. O Christ of God, we thank thee for thy forgiveness and guidance. Help us to learn of thee. Keep us close to the influence of thy love and within hearing of thy voice.

O Master of the good life, teach us to minister instead of waiting to be ministered unto, until we find our life in thy joy and likeness. Send us forth day by day as those who know that thou didst become flesh to live redemptively on this earth. Keep us confident in discipleship wherein we die unto self and live unto thee. Preserve us from jealousy of the gifts and attainments of others. Unite our differing talents in the doing of thy will. Reveal the times in which we are to stand in faith or when we are to venture boldly in thy name. Send us to the fields of humanity where we shall enter into the struggle between heartache and joy, shame and honor, despair and hope.

O Christ, bring guidance to those whose minds are estranged from goodness by sins and evil passions. Set the hearts of our youth on fire with adventure in holy things. Bless those who teach little children. Steady the feeble and uncertain. Show thy glory to the faithful. We would look unto thee, thou Author and Finisher of our lives, until we see thee face to face, beyond the trials and sufferings of our earthly days, and inherit the joy and fellowship which we have seen from afar; through Jesus Christ our Lord. AMEN.

77

HARVEST HOME FESTIVAL

Gracious and everlasting God, who art the Giver of all good and the Fountain of every blessing, who sustainest every living thing and guidest everything according to its season; all glory and praise be unto thee for thy abounding goodness. Thy faithfulness is from generation to generation.

Every morning thy mercies refresh us, and each evening they bring renewal. Heaven and earth are bathed in thy splendor and beauty. Thou hast filled the life of each of thy children with the gifts of thy Spirit. The fleeting days of our life are a reminder that thou art the great Reaper and dost keep all thy promises. For all thy goodness and mercy, hallowing and pursuing our lives, we give thee our heartfelt thanks.

O Thou who hast taught us not to live by bread alone but by every word that proceeds from thee, we would praise thee for Jesus Christ, thy richest Miracle of heavenly grace. In him we behold the fruits of thy saving righteousness and love. Forgive us our sins of barrenness in faith and sympathy. Make us generous in sharing our many undeserved blessings. Give to each of us the roots of faith, the tendrils of hope, and the blossoms of love so that abiding in Christ we may bear much fruit in thy kingdom.

We thank thee that thou dost scatter thy good seed upon the soil of every heart. Thine is an eternal harvest, and neither the coldness of evil nor the frost of sorrow can extinguish the warmth of thy redeeming love. Gratefully do we lift up our spirits this morning for those who have been good witnesses unto thee in and out of season, who in time of suffering bore the fruit of patience and faithfulness, and who in hours of hardship sank their roots of life deeply into thy Spirit. We rejoice that through their labors and endurance thou hast revealed that thou art faithful as thou sowest and reapest the harvest of thy kingdom.

Fill us all with the inspiration of this sacred hour that we may walk humbly and obediently in thy holy way. Inspire thy church to become one with thy will, strong in the midst of evil and courageous to proclaim thy gospel. Unto thee, O God, who in Christ art Lord of the harvest, be honor and glory, world without end. Amen.

78

WORLD COMMUNION

Holy and gracious God, who didst so love the world that thou gavest thine only-begotten Son that whosoever believeth in him should not perish but have everlasting life; we come to thy table as guests with people of every race and clime. Not one of us can trust in our own righteousness. We need the gifts of saving forgiveness, of restoring goodness, and of healing fellowship. In penitence and sorrow do we acknowledge our sins which divide us from one another. We confess that we have not heeded thy pleading love that went to the cross as an eternal sacrifice for us. Strengthen us with power through thy Spirit in the inward man, that Christ may dwell in our hearts through faith, that rooted and grounded in love we may with all the saints in heaven and on earth know the vastness and the inclusiveness of the love of Christ which passeth knowledge.

Thou Saviour and Shepherd of all, pour out thy Spirit upon thy Church universal even as thou art its living Head. Remember in thy mercy all who join us in worship and in breaking of bread; all who teach, heal, and preach in the name of the gospel; all who suffer or endure hardship for their faith; and all who wait for the hand of compassion.

We bring before thee our prayers for all enemies of thy Word and for all who are blinded by the gains of the world. Be thou as gracious unto them as thou hast been unto us. Meet them with a soul-stirring experience that beholds the light of an eternal justice and love.

We bring before thy comforting presence those in our midst to whom the sorrow of death has come, those who suffer from sickness, those who are sorely tempted or are filled with anxiety. Restore unto each the joy of thy salvation.

Let our communion with thee, our living Lord, cause us to yield ourselves to thee that we may henceforth live as those who are not their own, but as bought with a price. Glory be unto thee, O Christ, who livest and reignest forever, world without end. AMEN.

79

OVERARCHED BY AN EVERLASTING MERCY

O Lord our God, who art the Father of us all and who controllest all things; we wait in thy sanctuary to be filled and renewed by thy gracious Spirit. Direct our praying with a power from on high. We rejoice in this worship, for in thee do we live and move and have our being. To thee belong all praise and honor for the countless blessings of our life. Thy beneficence has supported and disciplined us, rebuked and counseled us, guided and chastened us, strengthened and saved us. Above all do we thank thee for the revelation of thyself in Jesus Christ, thy Son and our Lord. In him thou didst come to bring forgiveness of sins to those who in faith and repentance lift their desires of life unto thee. Because thy holy righteousness is overarched by an everlasting mercy, thou dost not cast us off. Thy holy Spirit renews the contrite and guides the humble.

Father Almighty, who carest for all thy children; we intercede for all whose life is dear to us that they also may receive the joy of knowing life through the insights of faith. May they not look at our wrongdoing which often causes us to hurt those we love most. Give them to behold the intentions of our hearts which outreach what we are. Make us understanding and forgiving with all men. May the spirit of forbearance and of patience govern us. Help us to discover the opportunities in which we may share the mind of Christ.

We pray for those in places of leadership and of responsibility in our land; for all teachers and inspirers of youth; for those engaged in the ministry of healing; for all who guide the affairs of business and for those who toil in office, factory, or home. Touch us with a sense of kinship with the frail and the forgotten of our kind. Thou desirest ever to work through each one of us to fashion a holy pattern of life; make us unto thee as clay in a potter's hands.

Unite us with the fellowship of faith throughout the world so that having been comforted and strengthened by thy grace, we may share the blessings of suffering and the fruits of joy with all who lift up their hearts unto thee; through Jesus Christ our Lord. AMEN.

80

10/13/57

THINE IS THE POWER AND GLORY

O God, who in Christ art our glorious Ruler and our saving Life; thy steps measure the planets, thine eyes are swift to see the needs of thy children. We come to thee out of the daily round of life, each with a full measure of praise. Where monotony filled our spirits, we were revived by the beauty and loveliness in the world and in the lives around us. When our minds were fretful and inclined to self-pity, thou didst open our eyes to the lowliness of our Master and Lord. Thy commandments have been signs along the way for us. Thy Spirit has empowered us to love and to endure. Above all, when we were discouraged and found that there was no good thing within us, thou didst come with the mercy of forgiveness and of inward renewal. For all thy love we would love in return. For all thy secret ministries we offer thee our praise.

We entreat thee, our Father, on behalf of all who plan and work for peace in the world. Bestow thy Spirit's wisdom and courage to use for the common good the vast physical energies which are disclosed through science. Let no one seek easy or selfish solutions to our problems which would force people to surrender their birthright of freedom. Give us the faith that thine is the power and the glory.

We implore thy consolations of everlasting life upon those who have lost loved ones and stand in lonely and heavy days. We beseech thee to bring a cup of strengthening to those who must make difficult decisions and who wrestle with temptations. Give them right judgment and hold before them the rewards of the good life.

Gracious God, without whom nothing is good; in time of prosperity let us not forget thee: make us thankful; in adversity let us not become bitter: awaken thou trust; in suffering let us not despair: make us strong. When others speak evil, keep us serene and aid us to speak good; when others receive blessings, save us from envy and make us glad; when others have a hard way, help us to surrender ease and make us burden-bearers. O Christ, help us to stand or fall for thy sake, who with the Father and the Spirit livest and reignest forever and ever. AMEN.

81

NATIONAL MISSIONS

Our Father, who art Lord of the harvest of souls; we thank thee that thou hast sown thy Word abundantly in our nation. We praise thee for all our forefathers who refused to govern without acknowledging thee and who made laws in the spirit of thy commandments. We are grateful for all who in establishing farms, villages, and cities also built churches to confess their faith in thy holy will.

We beseech thee, O gracious God, to awaken within us the zeal of love to proclaim the gospel of salvation in our nation. Give us compassion for the shepherdless multitudes and help us to bring a ministry of guidance, comfort, and healing to them. Endue us with loving patience to consider the misery and hopes of the underprivileged. Fill us with holy impatience where in our land children and youth are withheld from the Master by the influence of evil, ignorance, or poverty. Unite our efforts and prayers with those of all races as they enrich our common heritage and await a brotherly hand and heart more than riches.

O holy Spirit of God, breathe upon us such disturbing and saving power that we, as members of the body of faith, shall behold the Christ beckoning us beyond pulpits and altars to come into the field of humanity ripe unto spiritual harvest. Forgive us if in our own joy and fellowship we have forgotten the wider circle of concern where thy Spirit is working. Help us to rise above the walls of self-interest and make us pioneers of faith and love in the kingdom. Give us generous hearts which recall the Saviour's gift of life for all.

Strengthen laymen and ministers, and all leaders of our church, in the founding and establishing of new churches and fields of service. Let not difficulty or disinterest keep them from seeing the resources of the Spirit. We would remember that to whom much is given, of him much will be required. Baptize thy church with the prophet's fervor and with a love for the gospel until believing hearts release a new spirit of righteousness and men everywhere rejoice in thy salvation; through Christ our living Lord. AMEN.

82

AUTUMN FLIGHT

O God our Father, who in Jesus Christ hast given us the wings of eternity; we thank thee that thou hast placed into our being the homing instinct of the soul. We praise thee for the church, teaching us the knowledge that in the seasons of joy and of sorrow, of life and of death, we belong to thee. As the birds fly southward in this autumn, so may we be drawn by the life and spirit of thy kingdom. Sound the directions of the kingdom before us that we drift not among evil winds. Lift us in hope to soar above the clouds of despair.

Lord our God, without whose knowledge not a sparrow falleth; forgive us for not trusting thy lovingkindness. We confess that, like small children, we have compared our gifts with others' and so have forgotten thy mercy which bestowed our abundance. In blindness we have withheld for ourselves what thou dost intend for all members of thy family. The things of earth have often kept us from ascending to the heights from which we may see our brothers and sisters throughout the world. Embrace us with thy love that we may pursue with all thy children the life that is in Christ.

Gracious Father, we praise thee for leaders in the wisdom of love and for guides in the paths of mercy. Give us this day the grace so to follow thy Spirit's leading that we may strengthen the brethren. Place in our breast the spirit of compassion to come in thy name to the homeless and to the innocent victims of devastation and injustice. Help us to give them security against the cold and hunger of a winter that blows against body and soul.

O thou Companion of us all, lead us on the course which in Jesus Christ thou hast set before us. Fill us with the song of joy. Thou who wouldst have none lose their way, guide us safely through the days and nights, through summer and winter, until at last our flight through this world brings us forever close to thee; through Jesus Christ our Lord. AMEN.

83

REFORMATION DAY PRAYER

O Thou unchanging and merciful God, whose glory and truth endure unto all generations; we praise thee for thy grace in Jesus Christ, freely offered unto all people. On this festival of the Reformation we thank thee that thou dost answer our deep search and hunger of faith with an assurance of the gift of thy righteousness and love. Thou comest to commune intimately with each of us, thy children. Thou speakest thy word of forgiveness to every penitent soul. Thy power of new life fills each believing heart that waits for thee. We adore thee, Lord of the Church, our only Mediator and Redeemer.

Our Father, with deep gratitude do we acknowledge the heroism and courage of those who have kept the faith in times of darkness and persecution. Thou hast inspired prophets and apostles, martyrs and leaders, where people yearned for the liberty of the Spirit. Thy Spirit, O Christ, hath cleansed hearts and temples of pride and error. Enter thou the doors of our worship and devotion, thou true High Priest of God's salvation. Form and reform us into healthy and obedient living temples of thine.

Lord of the Church, open our eyes to every temptation within and without her fellowship. Save her from presumptuously withholding thy free gifts. Keep her from the arrogance of bestowing promises which thou only canst make to a repentant and believing heart.

O Shepherd of faith, who wouldst have thy church to be one flock; forgive our strife and divisions. Lead us with charity toward all that we may keep the bond of unity in the spirit of peace. Thou who wouldst have all men come to the knowledge of truth and to find peace in thee, give us grace to witness with courage and joy in thy name.

O Christ, let the authority of thy Church be thy love; may her power be in thy Spirit; may her influence be through consecrated lives; may her teachings be thy Word; may her mission be the proclamation of thy gospel; may her greatness be a humble confession and her splendor a losing of self in thy kingdom. Make us as disciples today, worthy heirs and stewards of the life, faith, and trust in our keeping. Now unto him who worketh far more abundantly than anything that we ask or think, be glory in the Church by Christ Jesus through all ages, world without end. AMEN.

84

SPEAK, LORD, FOR THY SERVANT HEARETH

O God, the heavens are telling thy glory and the earth proclaims thy handiwork; speak unto us in the hush of this hour, that we may hear the voice of thy Spirit. Thou hast assured us in Christ that thou hast yet many things to say unto us. Make us eager to hear what thou sayest about our ways and for our day.

We praise thee, O Lord, for thy voice of beauty in swirling leaves, rustling trees, splashing raindrops, and clean winds. We thank thee for every precious melody of the past and for every sound whereby our heart is quickened and gladdened. We are grateful above all for thy voice of saving love and of searching goodness in Jesus Christ. As he speaks to the humble and to the proud, we hear the accents of the Eternal. Whether his voice calls or reproves, we hear thy everlasting greatness echoing through the temples of the ages down to this very hour in which we pray. In him we hear the quick sound of tenderness and the low note of compassion. Sharpen the hearing of our consciences to catch thy clear voice among the cries of lust, prejudice, and self-will.

O Christ, as thou callest us by name, we confess that we have wandered far from thee in thought, will, and deed. We have not heeded thy voice of warning as it recalls for us thy commandments, thy righteous ways, and thy judgments. We have often spoken proudly when we should have listened. Forgive us our sins, O God, and unite us in a new song with all believers in the glorious harmony of thy Spirit.

In the confused clamor of our day give guidance to the leaders and members of thy church everywhere. Whisper hope to the sorrowing and disconsolate. May some accent of thy truth be like the sound of a silver bell to hardened or unbelieving hearts. Let the proclamation of thy Word be thy voice to us this day.

Thou who dost speak even more loudly in the silence than thunder in the night, commune with those seeking thy truth in the strife with falsehood, seeking reconciliation with one another, or seeking strength in time of suffering. Now let the words of our mouths and the meditations of our hearts be acceptable in thy sight, O Lord, our Strength and our Redeemer. AMEN.

85

DEDICATION

Eternal God, who hast set in man's heart the desire to build altars of sacrifice and temples of praise; we thank thee for this holy place of worship. We rejoice in thy blessings lavished upon us as a congregation. Thou hast shared with us the glorious gospel of salvation through him who is the Lord of the Church. Thou hast inspired our hearts to love thee, our wills to serve thee, and our minds to seek after thy truth. But above all, thou hast knit our lives in the fellowship of faith with thee and one with another. Now thou wouldst lead us into new experiences in the midst of the beauty of holiness.

We thank thee, O God, that where people mingle in great multitudes and with many needs, our church may serve in thy name. Amid the busy movement of the city its spire points quietly to the City of God. Above the noise of daily toil its bell peals forth thy praise. Where tension and haste corrode the souls of men, its doors invite to a holy peace. Its altar bids us seek thy forgiveness and reconciliation with our fellow man. The word we hear calls us to lay up treasures where neither moth nor rust doth corrupt, and to seek the riches of life and truth in thy kingdom.

We thank thee, O Christ, for thy servants whose vision and fidelity are wrought into our church. We are grateful for all who have planned and builded with faithfulness and skill. We praise thee for thy ministers and leaders who have inspired us in each generation. We are thankful for the generosity which thou hast put into the hearts of many so that this place of worship, love, and service could come into being. We adore thee for the memory of those whose faces we see no more but whose spirit is enshrined in our hearts. We praise thee for all the great host of witnesses by which we are compassed about. Hear us as each one consecrates himself to thee anew.

Grant unto thy church, O God, a new sense of thy power and a holy passion to glorify thee among all men and to let thy kingdom come and thy will be done; through Jesus Christ our Lord. AMEN.

86

STEWARDSHIP OF LIFE'S GIFTS

O Lord our God, who in divine graciousness invitest all and forgettest none, and who fillest a cup of blessing for thy household reaching from heaven to earth; we voice the praise and gratitude of our hearts unto thee. Giver of all we have and enjoy, who can measure thy goodness and count thy mercies? Great is thy faithfulness, our Father!

In the face of thy providence we confess, O Lord, our disregard of others, our turning aside from opportunities to be useful, our unfair comparisons, our blindness to true joy of the Spirit, our clinging to things which thou canst not bless. We have withheld the flowering and fruitage of thy gifts by our barrenness in love. Forgive our looking at thy gifts without listening to thy Word which directs their use.

Pardon our lukewarmness as members of thy holy Church for which Christ died. Have mercy upon us, O God, and with thy forgiveness grant us saving strength for a life that shall be an offering of sweet sacrifice before thee.

Thou who hast given unto us thy Son Jesus Christ for our salvation, help us to discover the joy of giving. Grant us wisdom to render a good account of our talents. We acknowledge that we cannot keep long what we do not invest in the love and life of thy kingdom. Remind us, Lord Jesus, that we cannot touch our neighbor's heart with anything less than our own heart. Bless all whose Christian work we help make possible.

Our Father, inspire us to work and give in the measure that we have been blessed. Many of us have received treasures in the radiance of bright days; some of thy gifts have come to us in time of sorrow; sometimes thou gavest different and better gifts than we asked for; others among us have plucked the slow-ripening fruit of the years; still others have found the gems of faith after much wandering and long waiting. All of us are thine, and we owe unto thee life itself with all its precious settings as a heavenly diadem. Let us then by thy grace walk not as those who lose a sacred trust through lovelessness, but as those who honor thee with complete devotion and so gain life everlasting; through Jesus Christ our Lord. Amen.

87

HOLY COMMUNION

O holy Son of God, who gavest thyself freely to become the Son of Man, our Saviour; we praise thee that in this holy Supper we see thee anew as offering the Bread of Life to the hungry in spirit. We remember that thou didst die like a grain of wheat in order to rise again in the abundance of eternal life. As in grateful love and adoration we observe these outward signs of the Sacrament, be thou within us to cleanse and strengthen our hearts.

Here in thy unseen Presence that is marked by the cross, we find ourselves in the company of our sins and of the divine image thou desirest for us. Here we are in the presence of those whom we have hurt consciously and unconsciously; here we feel at one with the invisible fellowship of believers. In contrition we know ourselves one with all mankind needing salvation and also with all who have tasted the cup of thy goodness. Merciful Redeemer, reconcile us to one another and to thyself. We need thee to restore us into the family of thy children. Mold us into one body possessed of the spirit of humility and gratitude. Give us a faith which is willing to forgive and ready to love one another. Renew our consciences and let the purity and power of thy grace lead us from evil into holy devotion.

We would look often upon thee, our Lord, and remember that we need not fear to sacrifice in love. Through it we are saved by thee and with one another. Living in thee we need not fear sorrow or temptation. Thou forsakest us not in life or in death. Let every trembling soul, hiding that of which it is afraid, come to thy table of grace and love. Let it find there the cup that stilleth every thirst after righteousness and offers newness of life in thy kingdom. To this end baptize us with thy Spirit that we may live to thy glory and in thy joy; through Jesus Christ our Lord. AMEN.

88

MEMORIAL SUNDAY OF THE CHURCH
(All Saints' Day)

Ever-living God, whose love in Christ is from all eternity and who scatterest thy abundant blessings upon every generation of men; we stand in awe before thy mystery of the ingathering of souls in life and in death. While we dwell in the midst of time and sense, we cannot see our loved ones who have gone on to the mansions of light. Our feeble, halting steps cannot follow them now. Thou Conqueror over death, teach us to soar by faith until we behold the joy of an endless kingdom. Let us die unto sorrow, sin, and the imperfect. Make our brief life the beginning of endless love and praise. Give us a trust that knows that the dark movements crossing our lives are but the shadow of thy hand, leading us toward the enduring City, whose Maker and Builder thou art.

Holy Father of us all, we unite our praise of thee with the voices of generations of believers surrounding thy throne. Centuries of faith in thee, O living Christ, speak to us in this hour of sacred memory. Thy Spirit quickens us with strength from on high. Console thou those who grieve in a deep sense of loss or in the pangs of loneliness. Open windows of faith and awaken us to the boundlessness of thy glory surrounding the earthly dwelling of our souls.

We stand reverently and gratefully before the good example of all whose names are written in our hearts and those, known and unknown, whose memory is hallowed in thy church. We thank thee for the lines of sacrifice and courage which marked their faces and for the imprint of unselfish labor upon their hands. We are indebted to thee for their spirit of joy which shone through hardship and for their perseverance in time of temptation. We are humbled and inspired by their prayer and example. Their lips have been invitations to taste of thy mercy and goodness. Lord, our lives have been enriched beyond our deserving by saints and martyrs, by prophets and apostles, of every age. May we so commune in the spirit of their faith and life that as we dedicate ourselves anew to the unfinished and the fresh tasks before us, we may at last enter with the redeemed into thy Church invisible and glorious, where Christ reigneth forever and ever. AMEN.

VI

Special Prayers

89

A MORNING PRAYER

Ever-watchful God and Father, who art fairer than the morning; lift thou the light of thy countenance upon us. Thou who hast awakened the consciousness of life within us, let our first thoughts and words be in praise and joy of thee. As we look into the faces of our fellow men, cause our gladness in being thine to become apparent. Keep us from thoughtless words or harmful deeds. Help us to use well all time, strength, and talent which this day will unfold.

Preserve us from anger, greed, or lust and aid us to walk the path of purity and love with all whom we shall meet. As we remember the days of those who have gone before us and look toward the days of those unborn, reveal to us the sacredness and meaning of thy light which will bless and guide us today. May every gift which we enjoy alone or in fellowship be accounted for as a token of thy confidence in us. And when evening comes, may there be no regret as we look unto thee. May we surrender the day with gratitude for every good thing thou hast accomplished through us. We pray in the name of Christ our Lord. AMEN.

90

AN EVENING PRAYER

Almighty Father, who standest behind the shadows and whose care for us is as constant as the stars on high; receive us and all whom we love in thy keeping. Lift from our minds the burdens of our wakeful hours. Take from us any spirit of ill will, bitterness, or distrust. Forgive us where we have permitted sin to enter our conversation or imagination and where evil has found fulfillment in any act. Make us better for tomorrow through thy pardon and peace. Free us from worldly cares and grant us the gift of sleep.

Abide with those who must endure pain. Watch over those who weep tonight. Let the sick and feverish feel thy healing and calm. Abide with the wakeful; protect all who labor through the night in danger and in temptation. Assure those of fearful and perplexed spirits that with the light of morning thou wilt give new portions of wisdom and strength, sufficient unto the day.

As each night recalls for us the brevity of our life and each dawn gives the promise of an eternal morn, so let us put our trust in thee, that waking or sleeping, we may feel thee near and know ourselves as thine; through Jesus Christ our Lord. AMEN.

91

FOR THE DAY'S WORK

O God, thou divine Provider of every blessing, who hast ordained that through work we are to gain our daily bread; we thank thee for the strength and talents of mind and body. We praise thee for work which not only beckons us to labor with our hands or thoughts but challenges us to partnership with thee.

Protect us this day from physical and moral dangers. Help us to give a full and honest measure in that which we expend or create, buy or sell. Let us never forget that we shall deal this day not only with machines and production, with sales and profits, but also with lives whom thou dost love.

We implore thee, our gracious Companion, to make us as

an influence for good. Help us to treat those in positions above us with respect, those who labor beside us with esteem, and those beneath us with fellow feeling. Make us faithful in small and large responsibilities, and whatsoever we do, let us do it heartily as unto thee.

Should our tasks become dreary or burdensome, help us to whisper a prayer. Recall for us happier and lighter hours made possible through our work. Help us to remember when beauty and inspiration, leisure and friendship, lifted our spirits. Keep us humble and glad in work well done.

If we meet rudeness, grant us forbearance; if someone is inconsiderate, incline our hearts toward patience and cheerfulness. Guide us in spirit and in deed, in the known and in the unknown, in weakness and in strength, that at the beginning and the end of our days we may have labored in thee and not in vain; through Jesus Christ our Lord. AMEN.

92

FOR ABSENT LOVED ONES

O God, blessed Keeper of all thy children, who art present with each of us while we are absent one from another; we commend unto thy loving guidance all those who are near to our affections but separated from us by distance. Where they adventure in life and learning, be thou their sure Leader. Should danger confront them, take them in thy safekeeping. If temptations lure them to forget the bonds of true affection or invite them to enjoy a sinful pleasure, call to their minds the good things worthy of all wrestling and waiting.

Give them moral courage and spiritual strength in times of decision. As each draws near to thee, may we be drawn more closely to one another. Since we are prevented from speaking tenderly to one another, whisper thou a word of assurance to them. Let the blessings we have received from our loved ones and friends become an increasing treasury of devotion and service. Cause abundant blessings to return unto them. Shield them in time of trouble, until they overcome by faith. If it be thy will, hasten the day when we may be reunited in praise and thanksgiving; through Jesus Christ our Lord. AMEN.

93

FOR PARENTS

O God, who thyself art as a Father and Mother unto us; thou knowest our joy in the children whom thou hast given us. We are humbled that something of ourselves is a part of them through the mystery and wonder of creation and growth. We remember the rich heritage of the race and of faith that flows in our sons and daughters. As we feed and clothe these dearest lives, make us conscious of thy providence and aware that their bodies are temples in which thy Spirit is to dwell. Open our minds as thoroughfares of enduring wisdom, our hearts as the fountains of noble emotions, and our souls as windows of inspiration in thy name. May we count no sacrifice too great through which their lives gain Christian fulfillment. Help us to make the influence of love, of understanding, and of confidence so strong in our home that our children may be able to wield a brave sword of the Spirit when away from us. By thy grace bless our home with the doors of wholesome companionship. Give us grateful, generous, and kind hearts. Let trials and hardships become the occasions when our trust in thee molds the minds of the young. By thy mercy let our mistakes and faults be understood in the light of our best intentions. We would honor thee in the name of thy Son, who dwelt in an earthly home and brought the beauty of faith and the glory of thy love; even Jesus Christ our Lord. AMEN.

94

UPON THE BIRTH OF A CHILD

God our Father, we adore thee for this precious life thou hast given to our keeping. We thank thee for the joy and devotion his birth has awakened in our hearts. As this little one lies helplessly in our arms, thou dost call upon us to give him protection, care, and love. Thou who carriest the lambs in thy bosom, so prepare us to nurture and guide him in a faith and love which are close to thy Spirit. We dedicate this child and ourselves to thee. Bless us in our home and church that we may grow in grace and may discover the gifts of thy love; through Jesus Christ our Lord. AMEN.

95

TEACHERS OF CHILDREN

O Christ, our Teacher from God; we adore thee for coming to us with the divine wisdom of love. Open thou the eyes of our understanding to the truth of thy gospel. Thou who on a hillside didst lift up the blessedness of life in the kingdom, grant us grace to hold forth thy Word of life with diligence and joy. As thou didst teach by streams and lakes and in temples and boats, so may we come close to the experience of the children entrusted to us. May their hours with us be thy time in which we use every good means and all knowledge available to us. Above all, let our love and gratitude to thee bless our teaching. Keep us humble to learn what we must teach and courageous to teach what is right in thy sight. Weave thou our small efforts into the larger lesson of life and faith which comes as a sacred heritage through all teachers of thy church.

Make us patient and kind with those who learn slowly or who have not felt the benediction of a Christian home.

Turn thou any feeling of anger or discouragement into a willingness to prepare more fully and to seek help unashamedly. O master Teacher and Saviour of us all, reward thou all our devoted efforts with a thirst for knowledge after thee that our children, even as thou, may increase in wisdom and stature, in favor before God and all men. Forgive and complete our poor and halting efforts in so high a calling.

God of our fathers, lead us often to the source of secret springs so that as we drink of thy Word and rejoice in thy companionship, we may be taught and strengthened by thy Spirit; through Jesus Christ our Lord. AMEN.

96

FOR A GOOD CONSCIENCE

Holy God, who hast given us freedom to choose between good and evil; we thank thee for the gift of conscience by which we may discern thy laws and perceive the love of Christ. Thy image in us awakens a kinship with the eternal. Yet we dare not forget that thou seest what no man can see: the inner intent and that which our heart treasures. With forgiving mercy cleanse thou our judgments and in love strengthen what is good. In times of decision and evaluation lay upon us a holy awareness. Sharpen our feeling and understanding of the right. Set our conscience true to the directions of thy Word, as we worship and study or join in fellowship and prayer. Above all, give us holy excitement and keen courage in sensing what we ought to do. Then grant us the faith to come to thee for power to do it. May the love of Christ constrain us in every judgment and act in the shadow of our fellow man. So may we learn of the ways of thy law and the wonders of thy grace, leading us through good and evil, the temporal and the eternal, until we become possessors of divine righteousness which is our joy and salvation; in thy name, who alone art good. AMEN.

97

WHEN OUR BOATS SEEM SMALL

O God, Ruler over wind and wave; the boats of our lives seem small and are tossed about helplessly. We have lost our course. The strong currents of opposition and the blasts of hardship make the steering of our hopes and endeavors difficult. We see the shoals and rocks of unbelief threatening us. Mighty Lord, who hast built our frail vessels of life and showest us the directions to sail with the cargo of faith, hope, and love; give us anchors for our driven souls, until our spirits are calm and we may see clearly the stars of thy truth and the Sun of Righteousness in Jesus Christ. By thy grace forgive our sins of floundering disobedience and drifting distrust. Let no call in distress come to us in vain. Guide us on the true course, as we follow the chart and compass of thy Word, until we reach the harbor of eternal fellowship and each places into thy saving and loving hands a life that is precious to thee; through Jesus Christ our Lord. AMEN.

98

FOR AN EVIL MOOD

O God our Father, who canst renew a right spirit within us; free thou us from evil moods and depressed minds. When the heavens appear dark and we can see no good thing in the faces of those around us, drive out the evil spirits of distrust and contentiousness. Turn our thoughts from foolish imaginings and superstitions. Forgive our oversensitiveness and easy irritation. Let not empty self-righteousness keep our hearts barren. Let not bleak hours blot out the memory of thy goodness.

O Lord, having cleansed the rooms of heart and mind, send

us thy good Spirit, that we may think on the things that are true, lovely, gracious, and worthy of praise. Fix our attention upon the sorrow and gladness of others. Place a song into our souls that our despondency may yield to the rhythm of new interests and activities. Befriend our forebodings with words of trust. Aid us to speak an encouraging word to others, since our own moods have taught us the value of friendship. May any discomfort or wrong we endure for thy sake be transfigured with joy. May our spirits be set free, to be filled of thee, O Christ, our blessed Master. AMEN.

99

FREEDOM FROM THE CLUTCH OF EVIL

O Christ, who didst wrestle with temptation in the wilderness for forty days; give us courage to struggle with evil which has a dangerous hold on body and soul. We have been enslaved through uncontrolled indulgence. Our selfishness has distorted the craving and warning of our senses. Poisonous temptations have pleaded for our happiness but then brought death to our better selves. We have disappointed our dearest ones and our friends. Thou knowest our sin and weakness; we reach for thy hand of mercy to deliver us from the clutch of evil.

O God, who in Christ believest in us; we would surrender to thee. Let us not postpone the hour of holy change. We trust thee at this moment to give us power for our wills and strength for our bodies. Keep us from expecting a quick release from deep cravings, hardened into habit by long indulgence. Help us to see that large wounds heal slowly; the crooked is straightened with patience; the good tree bears fruit in its due season.

O thou Friend of sinners, we dare not trust ourselves apart from thyself. We want to hear thy voice often. Give us resistance born of faith, and power to follow a new course by our love for thee. Bring us into companionship with those who know the highest joys and satisfactions of life. Teach us to speak often of thy wondrous power. Good and gracious Lord, we are thy children, and we want to become wholly thine with all thou hast endowed. Thanks be unto God, who giveth us the victory through our Lord Jesus Christ. AMEN.

100

HEALTH AND HEALING

Our Father, whose almighty power possesses healing in its wings; be unto us in our sickness the great Physician in Jesus Christ. Thy healing mercies touch body, mind, and soul; cure us where we are truly ill. Thou who canst make all things new, let thy health-giving life flow into our being. Grant us the miracle of faith to see thy all-knowing providence in what thou givest and withholdest. With thee all things are possible. Give us grace to trust thee to work, openly and in secret, what is good for us in sickness as in health. Father, we would press our weakness close to thy strength.

O Christ our Lord, whose word stilled the stormy sea; quiet thou our troubled thoughts and feverish spirits that in the calmness of thy presence we may hear thee say, "Peace, be still." Impart wisdom to the doctors and let knowledge, medicine, and ministering hands become channels for thy healing and restoring mercies. O God, hasten the day when in new confidence we may return to thy temple to praise and thank thee for thy unending love and compassion toward us in Christ; to whom belongs all honor and glory. AMEN.

101

SUFFERING

Eternal God, who in Christ didst feel the pain and anguish of the cross; come unto us in hours of pain. Teach us the secret of thy endurance in the heat of suffering. Hold us securely when in agony we know not how to cling to faith and are weary of life. Grant us the vision of the strong Son of God as he beheld love and meaning shining upon the way of sorrows. By the same strength given in his suffering, we would await thy wise purpose and tender comfort.

Friend of the lonely, in sleepless hours we think of thee and remember how often we tasted with joy thy refreshing streams in days past. Thou who in Christ didst so quickly discern the sick and suffering among the multitudes wilt not forget us now. Fill our cup with new consolations and goodness, not tasted in happier days. Help us to recall the thousands who suffer in this world and the countless ones who pray for us. Let us become better followers of thine for having known thee in the darkness. Make us brave and thankful in thy redeeming life; through Jesus Christ our Lord. AMEN.

102

WHEN OUR TIMES DISMAY US

Father almighty, constant in wisdom and infinite in compassion; hear our prayer as we turn to thee because our times dismay us. Our hearts are fearful of the awful power thou hast placed in our hands. We behold the terror in the eyes of those who have been wounded by the horrors of destruction. We view soberly the madness of men seeking to save themselves by destroying the world. We confess that we have not always discerned clearly thy purposes which accompany every gift. Lord of all, who didst create order out of chaos and hast brought light and life into being; create order among the minds and spirits of men in our times. Share with us the privilege of beholding today that what thou hast made is good.

O God, be thou with us on unexplored ways. Make us brave to use the truths we know and unafraid of new truths. Let the spirit of wisdom, of love, and of trust accompany the mightiest and the smallest problems. Hold before us the vision of a day when the dreaded powers of darkness and the forces of destruction become subject to thy reign of righteousness. Teach us to transform the fathomless energies at our disposal into holy light and strength of service. When the sure movement of thy Spirit seems too slow against the pace of turmoil, teach us thy patience, O Christ. When our souls are cast down because the evil seems stronger than the good, lead us to hope in thee. O Lord, thou ordainest the orbit of the atom and the pathway of the stars; thou canst surely guide our little lives and our confused days with a wisdom that is eternal; through Jesus Christ our Lord. AMEN.

103

IN TEMPTATION

O God, our Friend and Saviour, who hast promised that in every temptation thou wilt also give the strength to overcome; deliver us from the grip of sins which entice us. Help us to see clearly the ugly and harmful consequences which the allurements of evil seek to hide. Expose those temptations which clothe themselves in our own desires and pose as our need. Give us the imagination to behold the lives of those who may be harmed or saddened if we succumb to the attractions of sin. Hold before us the steady joy of a pure heart against a short-lived, wicked rapture. Restrain us from overconfidence which risks foolishly in dangerous associations a good name, a holy bond, and sacred vows. Multiply our strength of resistance with each refusal to do evil. Open our eyes to behold the beauty of the Christian life. Awaken our senses to the delight of a clean body and mind. Fill our hearts with desires which leave not ashes of regret but bring life's fulfillment. Give us grace to form a friendship with every good thing that fortifies our souls. Most of all do we seek the strength that was revealed in Christ so that in our fierce wrestling with the flesh we may gain the glorious victory of the Spirit; both now and forevermore. AMEN.

104

FOR STRENGTH TO CARRY

O Christ, who as the Son of God didst reveal a divine will and power to bear the burdens of mankind; grant us grace to bear one another's burdens in thy love; give us strength to carry the burdens we ourselves are to bear with courage; bestow patience to endure the burdens which cannot be removed at this time; and grant us trust to cast into thy merciful hands those burdens which only thou canst lift from our souls, minds, and bodies; in the name of him who shall sustain us and whom we would glorify. AMEN.

105

A PRAYER FOR YOUNG PEOPLE

O God our Father, who hast given us the strength and the dreams of youth; we thank thee for every urge which causes us to search after thee. We would discover the wonder of thy ways. We are grateful for all who have prepared our homes and schools, and for all who inspire us to use our minds and wills in a noble adventure. When we see evil and misery in the world, we become discouraged. When we look at thee, O young Christ, we feel ourselves drawn out of narrow lives of ease into a life that is wide in love and service.

O Master and Friend, keep us from living carelessly within reach of evil we cannot resist. Let us be unafraid to stand against temptation, for thou hast promised us deliverance. Keep our hearts grateful. Fill our being with kindness, thoughtfulness, and joy. Make us ready to love those for whom no one cares. May purity in heart make us ready for holy tasks. May brave faith lead our minds to new truths. Make us to be honest and considerate companions who will be remembered as true followers of thine; in thy name. AMEN.

106

GRADUATION

O God our Father, who hast formed us in wisdom and hast made us to love and serve thee as thy sons and daughters; our hearts beat high in gratitude tonight. Thou hast given us minds through which to think thoughts after thee. We have bodies with which to respond to strength and joy in thy world around us. Thou hast given us hearts that we may have fellowship one with another. Above all, we have received souls that we may know thee, O eternal Spirit and Companion of our lives.

We are thankful for our parents and homes where we received the first knowledge of life and love; for our school and teachers who in patience and wisdom inspired us to seek after truth and learn the grace of living together; for this community and nation over which the flag of freedom and of brotherhood may fly; and for the rich heritage which we have received through books, friendship, work, and play. Go with us from here, our Father, upon unknown ways. Give us a firm faith that as we follow the things which are pure, good, and true, thou wilt use us in wondrous purposes. Make us brave against temptations which offer easy evil or would extinguish hopes and dreams. Bless us now and lead us into a life that shall become a hope and promise for a better world; through Jesus Christ our Lord. AMEN.

107

FOR FINDING OUR VOCATION

O God, who through the work of Christ our Lord dost seek to bless every calling; direct and prepare us as we seek the nature of life's work best fitted for us. Bestow thy Spirit that through our chosen vocation we may do the Father's will. Save us from accepting a form of livelihood whereby any life may be harmed or blighted. As thou callest us to follow thee, O Master, unfold for us the way in which our talents may multiply into faithfulness over many things. Make us receptive to thy guidance as we pray, study, and gain counsel.

Give us wisdom and courage to know ourselves. Empower us to evict conceit and daydreaming. Enrich us with the grace to discover the gifts implanted in our minds, bodies, and spirits. Thou art not a Friend of those who bury their talent. Make us unafraid of failures and wrong choices. Thou art ready to help us when we walk boldly by faith and adventure in new forms of service among our fellow men. Kindle our hearts until our striving and endeavor reflect thy Spirit. Give us tasks greater than our strength so that in calling upon thee for help, we may honor and praise thee as we labor with joy in thy kingdom; in the Master's name. AMEN.

108

A WEDDING PRAYER

Everlasting Father, who in Christ dost hallow all hearts joined in love; grant now thy blessing upon the holy vow spoken by these thy servants, that it may become an open door of faith and hope and love. May they take the Spirit of the sanctuary with them into their home. Fill their minds with grace to seek thy wisdom and purpose in every adventure of life together. Let thy Spirit rise upon them with the gifts of joy, generosity, and forbearance. Give them daily the skill of understanding and patience. May each seek to nurture and guard the other's trust and hopes.

Gracious Guest of home and heart, keep high the spirit of reverence within their minds so that they may be swift to appreciate, slow to blame, and wise to seek thy counsel. Keep them from evil. Imbue them with the power of faith that keeps us faithful in the things which are true and good. Let the light of thy presence enfold any sorrow, hardship, or temptation before them.

Lord of all our ways, quicken and strengthen the hearts of all who are bound together in affection and who in spirit and prayer share the holy beauty and heaven-laden promises of this hour. Bestow upon these who have now become one in life the spirit of fellowship that shall bind them together with all who love and serve thee, that they may forever be thine and one with thy family in heaven and on earth; through Jesus Christ our Lord. AMEN.

109

WHEN GOD SEEMS FAR AWAY

O God, who art ever-present, from whose Spirit we cannot flee and whose purpose we cannot evade; at times thou seemest far away. Hold us as a father holds his child. Forsakenness haunts us when time brings change and when friends leave us. Our goals become dim when life is hard and attainments are slow. Life seems fruitless as disappointments crowd in and our best efforts fail. The days before us appear barren and without promise. We are caught in circumstances, surroundings, and ties which offer no release. Dark thoughts follow us. Appear unto us, O God, like a light in the night.

Thou who hast put the thought of thyself in our minds and the hunger for thee in our souls wilt not elude us forever. Our eyes seek thy face, and our hearts reach out after thee. Thou dwellest not only in the heavens or in the reason and knowledge of man. Guide us in the reasoning and knowledge of faith which trusts thee where we cannot see. Thou art our Father and hast revealed thyself through Christ in the lonely and heavy hours of the human heart.

Grant us patience and courage to prepare ourselves during all hours for the holy moment when we perceive thee, that in welcoming thee into the shadows and brightness of our souls, we may find thou hast always been with us; through Jesus Christ our Lord. AMEN.

110

FOR THOSE GONE BEFORE

Our Father, who in Christ art the Resurrection and the Life, and who callest us to work while it is day ere the night cometh; we thank thee for those who, having served in this church in faith and love, are now dwelling in light and life with thee. We are grateful for the many ways in which they dedicated their talents in the work of this congregation—some in song, some through teaching, some as leaders, and many by their glad witness in worship and generosity. Comfort all who are in sorrow. May the faith and deeds of those who have gone before become good ground in which our devotion to thy kingdom bears fruit worthily and abundantly. Teach us that in hallowing precious memories, we are to look not back but forward toward him who meets us in life and in death, in this life and in the life to come; even Jesus Christ our Lord. AMEN.

111

IN TIME OF BEREAVEMENT

Our Father, who in Christ didst bring us the power of an endless life and who hast given us our loved ones; we trust thee though the music of life is stilled in a soul dear to us. Thou didst inspire the affection, joy, and faith we shared so intimately. Only thou canst understand our broken hearts and dost measure our grief. Thou, O Christ, hast known the darkness of death and the anguish of forsakenness. Thou hast heard our joint prayers in happier days. Speak thy word of Resurrection and Life unto us. Assure us of thy conquest over death and of the vigil of thy everlasting love for dear ones. Make the light of faith to shine through blinding tears. Let the echo of heavenly music in the gospel cause us to listen for thy unending song of triumph.

Lord of time and eternity, we thank thee for precious years and enriching companionship which united heart, mind, and endeavor. Let the hope we treasured shine down the future's broadening way. Cause the night of sorrow to be transformed into a waiting for the dawn of thy kingdom. Sanctify these hours of bereavement with thy presence, that we may follow thy leading through the valley of the shadow and rejoice in the glory of thy house forever. Let our dismay be changed into an awareness of a holy and wise will, encompassing our own. May the comfort of friends become a mutual witness of an invisible fellowship. As we contemplate the brevity of life, may we use our remaining days in reverence and obedience, looking to thy grace to heal our wounds and to reunite us in the joy of life everlasting; in the name of our living Lord. AMEN.

112

WHEN WE KNOW NOT WHAT TO ASK

Our Father, who in Christ hast taught us to pray and hast promised to hear and answer us in all conditions; let thy Spirit move among us, for words fail us and we know not what to ask. O Heart that speakest with every heart, teach us to be still and listen. If we hear not thy voice, let us feel thy presence. Direct us to pour out our hearts until they are empty. We are thine! Thou hast a plan for our lives in thy glorious kingdom. O Christ, let not our dullness or unbelief cause us to miss what thou offerest. Give us strength to surrender our self-will that we may find a holy will. We would begin now with thee. Lord, wilt thou then speak so that thy servant heareth. In thy name we ask it. AMEN.

113

FOR THE SHUT-INS

O God, whose strength sweeps through the hills and enters the secret chambers of our hearts; befriend us in our helplessness as we face solitary hours. When the battle of life seems more than we can endure, send unseen spiritual aid to fortify us. Thou wilt not give us more to endure than what we are able to command in faith and strength. Help us to submit in such a manner to our afflictions that some good may shine through and a victory of the spirit may be won.

The walls which confine us press heavily upon our thoughts. O Spirit of Christ, who didst appear behind closed doors; lift thou our minds and hearts and set them free.

When we are discouraged because we cannot work or move about, grant us the gentle grace of imagination to adventure in the world of beauty and thought. Make us quick in sympathy with all who are imprisoned, or bound by blindness, or held by deformity, or confined by mental darkness. Help us to pray often for all who need thy mercy.

Father, we thank thee for unlimited power to love and to be wholly thine. We are grateful that thou canst teach and inspire in the beauty of the sanctuary and in a room of suffering. Keep us faithful as thy disciples on the way thou hast given us. Lord, thou hast made our souls to love and to enjoy thee forever. Let any cross which is laid upon us bring our lives to their fulfillment through the grace which was in Christ Jesus, our Lord. AMEN.

114

FOR VITAL MEMBERSHIP IN THE CHURCH

Eternal Father, who in Christ hast given us the commandment that we love one another even as thou dost love us; grant that our membership in thy holy church may bear much fruit of the Christian life. Keep us growing with each prayer and deed. Where human frailties become apparent in our midst, prevent us from taking thy saving fellowship for granted. Reveal thy gifts among us. We are not our own, alone or together, for we have been bought with the price of thy redeeming love. We are indebted to heroes and martyrs for vision and sacrifice. O God, give us grace to follow valiantly in their faith and devotion, that being one in thee, we may speak a persuading word to a world divided against itself.

Make us ready to offer with joy the best talents and gifts. Make us humble and gracious. Let the faults and offenses of others become occasions in which we may prove our love and offer our help. Give us the right words when heartening and cheering words should be spoken. Let insight lead us to bring help to every form of distress. O Christ, empower us to seek those who are waiting to be invited into thy presence. Lord of an everlasting kingdom, hold thou the holy purposes of thy church before our every interest and endeavor, that we may be a worthy fellowship of disciples and a good leaven of the gospel in the world; through him whose name we bear. AMEN.

115

THE CUP OF JOY

God our Father, who through the birth of thy dear Son, our Saviour, hast brought boundless joy to every believing heart; let the radiance upon our faces, the gladness in our hearts, and the cheerfulness of our spirits reveal that we love thee. Help us to rejoice in the blessings and good gifts which come to all. Lead us to pure pleasures and make us glad in useful tasks. May our joy be accompanied by the melodies of praise and thanksgiving.

O Christ, who didst endure even the cross for the joy that was set before thee by the Father; forbid that we should permit outward conditions or misfortune to hide our joy in thee. Make us masters of circumstances and rulers of our dark moods. Let the irritability and distress of others reveal their need of cheer and help.

O Thou who art the Lord of joy, open for us the fountains of life wherein we find endless delight as we not only touch the cup of blessing with our own lips but press it to the lips of others and empty it in love and devotion until we enter into the everlasting joy of thy kingdom; in thy name. AMEN.

116

CHURCH WOMEN

O God our Father, who in Christ hast given us freedom and joy for living; set thou clearly before us the goals for life and love. We bless thee for the fellowship of Christian women in which we are called to let the beauty of the Christian life shine forth. We praise thee for the example of all who, having kindled our spirits, make our influence richer. We are glad in the kind of togetherness in the church which makes us count for so much more as individuals.

Let this season become fruitful for our souls. Sweep from our vision all darkness of self-love and the blur of doubt. Release within each of us the power which we see so fully in our Saviour and Lord.

Now grant unto women everywhere, bearing crosses for thy sake or waiting for the promise of a new day, the knowledge that thou art a strong Deliverer of the weak, merciful unto the humble, and a Giver of faith to those who seek thy grace; through Jesus Christ our Lord. AMEN.

117

CHURCH MEN

O God, who hast designed the world in wisdom and love; we rejoice that in Christ thou dost call us to be fellow workers with thee. In his presence we know thy divine friendship, forgiveness, and strength. His hands bless us in our toil; his thoughts pursue us in our deliberations; his Spirit calls us to a new manhood in the kingdom.

Father, thou knowest how we face daily the patterns of evil and their temptations to surrender high principles. Hold before us thy love in Christ and give us courage. The good we want to do often escapes us. The evil we do not want to do becomes our companion. Forgive us our sins and free us so that we may walk and serve as thy disciples.

We thank thee for the inspiring and strengthening fellowship of the church. Widen and deepen the effectiveness of our prayers and service because we have thought together upon thy will. Light the lamps of our imagination so that we may uphold the arms of thy servants and strengthen the brethren. When we stand alone and our faith and love are tested, recall for us our holy bond with those who have been steadfast in thee.

Make us to be a blessing in our community. Let us be a source of joy and confidence in our homes. May not the cares of the world and the deceitfulness of riches stunt our growth in the Christian life. May we stand in the faith and be strong as God's men; in the name of our Elder Brother, even Jesus Christ our Lord. Amen.

118

MOTHERS AND DAUGHTERS

Gracious God, who in Christ didst come to us in a humble home; we praise thee this night for the faith and love of our mothers. We thank thee for thy Spirit's strength while they cared for us, taught us our first prayers, and guided us in the way of Christ. Bless thou the aged mothers with the consolation of thy mercies and the rewards of faith. Comfort those who are motherless and give us open hearts for those who need help to keep tender ties together.

Father, we thank thee for our daughters and the joy they have given us. Grant them the nobility and beauty of thy Spirit. Now bless our fellowship here in the name of the church we love, and make us one with all dear to us in heaven and on earth; through Jesus Christ our Lord. Amen.

119

FATHERS AND SONS

O God our Father, whom we know and love through Jesus Christ, thy Son our Lord; we are grateful this night that thou hast blessed us through our fathers. Their care and protection have strengthened us in growth and love. Their faith has inspired us to look unto thee. Their concern for us has nurtured us in brotherly trust and understanding.

We also thank thee for our sons, O Lord, and for the joy they have given us. May our influence cause them to give their hearts unto thee. Keep them from evil. Bless them with grace and wisdom. May the fellowship and faith within our church lead them into the gentlest and strongest manhood that was in Christ. Let us never forget the aged and the orphaned. Make us worthy to be called fathers and sons who honor thee in all their thoughts and ways; through Jesus Christ our Lord. AMEN.

120

WORTHY INSTRUMENTS

O God our Father, we thank thee that thou hast fearfully and wondrously made each one of us, thy children. May holy purposes direct us, the love of Christ constrain us, and the strength of the Spirit support us to be worthy instruments in thy kingdom. Teach us to walk with confidence and not without humility, with eagerness and not without consideration, with courage and not without reverence. Give us purity in heart when evil surrounds us. Make us brave to prune what is fruitless. Help us to cultivate what is good in thy sight. Increase our helpfulness as we touch the hands of our brethren. So enlarge our usefulness as thy hands bless us, until we lay down the unfinished tasks on earth and by thy grace are fashioned into perfect instruments of love and praise in everlasting glory; through Jesus Christ our Lord. AMEN.

121

PATRIOTIC MEETING OF FAITHS

Eternal God our Father, who hast made us for fellowship that reaches to the ends of the earth; we thank thee for every gift which becomes richer as we share it and more secure as we guard it one for another. We praise thee for the spirit of liberty thou hast entrusted and established through our fathers. Grant that we, their children, may prove ourselves mindful of thy favor and ready to do thy will for a new day.

Give us the grace to treasure the diversities of gifts within thy kingdom. Unite us in thy cause of righteousness, love, and peace. Save us from hatred, violence, and confusion. Set us firmly against cruel and heartless discriminations and against racial prejudice. Preserve us from arrogance and bigotry which pose as thy champions but lead blindly into intolerance and leaden-eyed obedience.

Enrich thou our meeting of minds and hearts this day that we may catch a vision of a greater destiny and the call of holy responsibility. Make us one in thee, and we shall be one with another; in the name of him who is the Way, the Truth, and the Life. AMEN.

122

OPENING PRAYER FOR A CITY COUNCIL MEETING

God of our fathers, thou who hast through the years given unto us the strength to build this great city; grant unto us the humility and wisdom to acknowledge that we cannot build enduringly unless we honor thee.

Give unto each of us an awareness of the many people in all walks of life who rely upon us to serve the common welfare and who trust us where they do not see.

Help us to be true to the highest hopes of the past. Share with us the vision of the City of God. Let not the still, small voice of conscience be stifled by the loud demands of the selfish, nor by the harsh utterances of the heartless.

Save us from violence, discord, and confusion, from pride and arrogance, and from every evil way. Defend our liberties. Let our strength become a blessing to the weak, and let our resources be at the command of all who are worthy, regardless of class, creed, race, or national origin.

May we so labor together that all may see our faces as set toward thee and as brothers. We ask it in the name of Christ, whose presence is in every street, in every home, and in all our affairs. AMEN.

123

PRAYER AT COUNCIL OF CHURCH WOMEN DINNER

Father, we thank thee that this beautiful day is crowned with the glow of fellowship in thy name. We praise thee for the united Christian heritage that has come to womanhood. Above all do we thank thee for the gospel, as it speaks with hope to every man, woman, and child in the communities of the world. Make each woman through our Council of Churches a sister in charity, a mother of faith, and a handmaiden of the Lord.

Bind us together, so that our gentleness may become a power for thee, our influence may be the spirit of love, and our beauty may be the touch of thy grace. Make this meal a symbol of our common need of thee and of our willingness to offer strength for thy work; through Jesus Christ our Lord. AMEN.

124

GRACE AT MEALTIME

Our Father, we thank thee for this food which thou hast provided so bountifully. May our eyes see thy grace within all gifts; let our lips be ready to partake and to praise; may our hands, as they reach out to receive, be ready to share. Grant us strength in all things to serve thee; through Jesus Christ our Lord. AMEN.

125

GRACE AT MEALTIME

Our Father, in the beauty of this evening fellowship we thank thee for thy presence in our midst. We are grateful for the bountiful gifts upon our table and for the gracious gifts which we hold in our hands, our minds, and our hearts. Bless us with the spirit of gladness tonight. Deepen our friendship with one another and our love for thy church; through Jesus Christ our Lord. AMEN.

126

A COLLECT FOR THE CHRISTIAN LIFE

O Christ, who in humility and faith didst trust the power of the Father's love and didst fearlessly and in compassion endure death upon a cross for our sake; grant that we may so love thee and thy kingdom that witnessing, laboring, and enduring in thy name, we may be known as thine in life and in death, and inherit the joy which thou didst behold and promise in our Father's kingdom. AMEN.

INDEX

Figures refer to prayer numbers.

130